Delicious
MORNINGS

Delicious MORNINGS

COMFORTING BREAKFASTS BAKED FROM SCRATCH

DINA FOGLIO CROWELL

Front Table Books
An Imprint of Cedar Fort, Inc. • Springville, Utah

ISBN: 978-1-4621-1460-3

Published by Front Table Books, an imprint of Cedar Fort, Inc.
2373 W. 700 S., Springville, UT, 84663
Distributed by Cedar Fort, Inc., www. cedarfort. com

Library of Congress Cataloging-in-Publication Data

   Crowell, Dina Foglio, 1974–
   Delicious mornings / Dina Foglio Crowell.
      pages cm
   Includes index.
   ISBN 978-1-4621-1460-3 (acid-free paper)
   1. Breakfasts. I. Title.
   TX733.C774 2014
   641.5'2—dc23
                          2014024252

Cover and page design by Bekah Claussen
Cover design © 2014 by Lyle Mortimer
Edited by Rachel Munk

Printed in the United States of America

10 9 8 7 6 5 4 3 2 1

FOR MY FAMILY

Tristen, Ashlynn, Kayeden, and Brennen, who graciously sacrificed precious time with me and gave me space to write and create. And to my husband, John, who scarfed down everything I made, including the mess-ups, while giving me honest feedback. And to my dogs, Ollie boy and Finn, who slept faithfully by my feet in the kitchen and at my desk for four months straight.

CONTENTS

PRAISE FOR *DELICIOUS MORNINGS*

Dina has mastered the art of creating recipes that are straightforward and made from scratch. Not only are they delicious, but they are pretty enough to decorate any table! The breakfast recipes in *Delicious Mornings* are the kind of comforting dishes that would actually make me look forward to hearing my alarm go off every morning.

— JORDAN SWARD, *RECIPELION.COM*

Delicious Mornings is a fabulous collection of breakfast dishes with beautiful photos and easy-to-follow recipes that any home cook will enjoy making. Dina is a talented cook who creates truly mouthwatering recipes. This is definitely my new go-to cookbook for our Saturday morning family feast—or any other time I want to impress my guests!

— SHAUNA SMART, *THEBESTBLOGRECIPES.COM*

There's nothing like starting the day with a donut made with premium chocolate! Dina blogged a recipe using Lindt chocolate during the holidays last year, and we were thrilled with the results. We can't wait to try her recipes in *Delicious Mornings*.

— ANN CZAJA, LINDT MASTER CHOCOLATIER

ACKNOWLEDGMENTS

I would like to give a special thank-you to my parents, Jimmy and Lucy Foglio, for always encouraging me and standing by my side. They lift me up when I'm down, and their steady applause is what truly keeps me shooting for the stars. A special thanks to my photographer friends—you know who you are—for critiquing my photos and offering tips and guidance to help improve my most challenging shots. Your talent amazes me and I continue to learn a tremendous amount from all of you. And an extra special thanks to Andria Post who, from the kindness of her heart, graciously offered her editing expertise. I would like to thank the blogging community for their camaraderie and constant support while I was on a short hiatus writing this cookbook. Their guest posting kept my readers engaged, and their constant support and advice helped me in many ways. And, last but certainly not least, I want to thank my fabulous readers—my online community who faithfully tries my recipes, offers me feedback, and keeps coming back for more. Without you, *Buttercream Bakehouse* would be lost in the blogosphere without purpose. You, my readers, give my blog purpose, and I thank you every day for letting me step into your kitchens (albeit virtually) to share my recipes and inspire you to create beautiful and delicious masterpieces. I am continually humbled by every one of you. Thank you!

INTRODUCTION

What could be more comforting than to wake up to the scent of a delicious breakfast baking in the oven? It brings me back to my childhood, when blissful aromas floated through our house on the weekends, and our family slowed down and enjoyed a meal together. Baking a tasty breakfast from scratch for your family is a rewarding experience that doesn't have to be daunting. In this book you will discover how to produce the flakiest, melt-in-your-mouth biscuits that taste amazing smothered with homemade apple sausage gravy. I'll show you how to make light, airy, time-saving classic cinnamon rolls that are sweetly sticky and billowy soft—a family favorite at the Bakehouse, my little corner of the world, nestled in the suburbs in historic Fredericksburg, VA.

I'm a self-taught baker. That's right! No fancy culinary degree or resume working at high-end restaurants. I learned to bake from cookbooks and blogs, just like you likely did. I am obsessed with reading cookbooks. I pack cookbooks on vacations and trips to the pool, instead of romance novels. I even keep a pile of cookbooks on the floor next to my bed so I can flip through them before I turn in for the night. I'm a foodie at heart. I love to eat, cook, and write about food. Experimenting and cooking in the kitchen brings me a joy I can't explain. It's an exciting moment when my kids, who are picky eaters, devour a new recipe, smile, and ask for more. *Delicious Mornings* will teach you how to do just that—create delicious breakfast meals that your entire family will love.

My culinary craving began when my son, Tristen, was born in 1999. I wanted him to have the best birthday cakes ever created, but I couldn't afford to pay for one. I went to the library and checked out a cake decorating book and read it cover to cover. I bought a few cake decorating tools and made an amazing cake all on my own. I was smitten, and I couldn't wait to create more cakes. Luckily, I had three more kids and many chances to practice. And, with the requests of friends and family, who wanted me to make cakes for them, I opened Buttercream, a home-based cake decorating business that became my passion. I decided to start a food blog when my customers began asking how I made the buttercream taste so light and fluffy, or what my secret was to making my cakes so moist and light. With that, my blog *Buttercream Bakehouse* became a reality in 2010. My blog soon became a popular platform for exciting baked recipes. I was so enrapt in my kitchen, developing marvelous recipes, honing in my new found photography skills, and editing posts that I no longer had time for my cake business, so I decided to close the doors to Buttercream and, in 2012, I started blogging full time. The rest is history!

My promise to my readers is that I only share recipes that are tried and true and that I love to pieces. The same is true for *Delicious Mornings*. This book is full of exclusive recipes for delicious baked breakfast entrees and sides. To tantalize your taste buds even further, I also added my best pancake recipes inspired by popular desserts, like Bananas Foster Pancakes—no flame required. I'll even share my secret on how to make the perfect stack of pancakes. And I carefully tucked in a few delectable breakfast-inspired desserts for your indulgence.

I wrote this cookbook with you, the home baker, in mind. All the ingredients I use are simple and easy to find. You can bake an enjoyable breakfast for your family successfully, and I'm here to guide you every step of the way. The best part is that, if you have a question about a recipe, you can drop me a line on my blog, www.buttercream-bakehouse.com, to ask for help. I will get back to you as quickly as I can and will never leave any question unanswered. It really is simple to make breakfast from scratch, and the magnificent scent wafting through your house bright and early in the morning will be a memory that you and your family will never forget.

HELPFUL TIPS FOR SUCCESSFUL BAKING

MAKING THE PERFECT MUFFIN

We have all had those frustrating baking moments when muffins fall flat or become dry and heavy. That's not a tasty, appealing muffin. After years of experimenting, I have finally found the secret to baking a perfectly moist and puffy muffin. But first, let's talk about common muffin mistakes to avoid in your cooking.

COMMON CAUSES OF FLAT, DRY, AND HEAVY MUFFINS

OVERMIXING—Overmixed muffins will have a chewy and dry texture. Flour has gluten, and when dry ingredients are mixed with wet ingredients, the gluten is immediately released. If over-mixed, it will overwork the gluten, giving the dough elastic texture which is delicious in a pizza crust, but not so much for a moist and delicious muffin. For tender, moist muffins, combine the dry ingredients separately from the wet ingredients, and then fold the two mixtures together, always adding the wet ingredients to the dry ingredients. To fold them together, use a large mixing spoon to cut down the center of the mixture, and then bring spoon back up to the top. It's a down, across, up, and over motion. Turn the bowl while folding, and stop once the batter is just combined. Some flour streaks should still be visible. When folding, make sure to scrape the bottom of the bowl and sides to incorporate all the flour. If you overmix the batter by mixing until all the flour is incorporated, your muffins will have peaks, tunnels, and a tough texture. Lumps of flour are good—leave them be!

INCORRECT MEASURING—It is also important to measure your dry ingredients accurately when baking. There are two ways you can do this. One option is to use a dry ingredient measuring scale. This scale will measure your ingredients by weight and will always give you exact measurements. Always use dry measuring cups when measuring flour. If you do not plan on using a measuring scale, the best way to add flour to a measuring cup is to fluff your flour prior to using it, and gently transfer it to your measuring cup with a spoon. Then take the back of a knife and smooth the top. Do not scoop your measuring cup into a packed bag of flour. This will add over 20% more flour than the recipe calls for, causing dryness and heaviness in your muffins.

TEMPERATURE—Use an oven thermometer to maintain the correct oven temperature, or your muffins may overbake and become dry. Temperature is the ultimate secret for a puffy muffin top. Some people like their muffins with a puffed dome, a classic characteristic of bakery-style muffins. This dome is created by cooking the muffins at the correct oven temperature. We're talking 400 degrees hot! Setting your oven at a hot temperature will set the outer edges of your muffin quickly, creating a burst of steam in the center that will lift through your muffin straight to the top. This will give you a glorious puffy muffin top. After 6–8 minutes, set the oven back to the temperature called for in the recipe, usually 325–375 degrees. Your muffin will continue to bake evenly at a proper muffin-baking temperature. In this book, some of the muffin recipes are baked in a cupcake pan instead of a muffin pan. Follow baking directions accordingly and you will have the most delicious, moist, and fluffy muffins!

THE SECRET TO A PERFECT STACK OF PANCAKES

These rules will help you make the perfect stack of pancakes. Making pancakes is very similar to making muffins, since the key is to work with the gluten in the flour so the pancakes cook properly. Unless otherwise noted in the recipe directions, follow these tips for a successful stack every time.

»   Preheat your griddle to 375 degrees, or heat a nonstick skillet over medium heat.

»   Mix the dry ingredients together, and then add fruit or toppings if the recipe calls for it.

»   Mix the wet ingredients separately and add them to the dry mixture. Fold until just combined. The batter will be lumpy. Do not overmix the batter.

»   Pour ¼ cup of the batter into the greased, hot griddle, using a ¼ measuring cup or large cookie scoop.

»   Flip the pancake when bubbles start to form on top, and the bottom edges are lightly golden brown. Do not press your pancakes while cooking.

»   Once flipped, cook the pancake for just a minute longer, or until it is lightly golden brown and the batter is no longer seeping from the sides.

»   Place the cooked pancakes on a wire cookie rack to cool slightly. Do not stack the pancakes on top of each other, since this will continue to cook them, and the steam makes them soggy.

GENERAL COOKING TIPS

I t's important to be incredibly organized while baking or cooking a new recipe. Do this by reading the recipe from beginning to end so you fully understand what you are about to do. It's also wise to take out all of your ingredients and measuring cups needed prior to starting. If food needs to be diced, sliced, or chopped, do this before you begin cooking. Then you can concentrate on following the directions, keeping your eye on the temperature and cooking time. Speaking of temperature, always use a preheated oven, hot griddle, or skillet. Use an oven thermometer for proper oven temperature, since some ovens are hotter than others. Mine has hot pockets, and I know that the left side cooks faster than the right side. Know your oven to ensure successful baking. When using pans, make sure you use what the recipe calls for. Dark seasoned pans will cook differently than bright, shiny aluminum pans or glass dishes. Spray your pans with the right cooking spray. Cooking spray with flour is used in baked goods, while cooking spray made without flour is used for eggs or savory recipes. Always position your oven rack to the middle unless otherwise noted. And, as always, use the freshest eggs and ingredients you can find. I never use imitation extracts, and I recommend that you do not use them either. The flavor will simply not be the same without the real extract. The same goes for herbs. Always used fresh herbs when the recipe calls for it. Your taste buds will thank you.

BASIC INGREDIENTS USED IN THIS BOOK

All baked goods will rise higher, taste fluffier, and taste better if the cold ingredients you use are at room temperature. For eggs, place them in a measuring cup of hot water for 3 minutes before using. If a recipe indicates milk and sour cream at room temperature, try leaving the ingredients out for an hour before assembling, or microwave the ingredients for 20 seconds, stir, and repeat until they reach room temperature.

TYPES OF FLOUR—There are two types of wheat found in flour—hard and soft. The difference between them is the amount of protein they contain. Hard wheat is higher in protein, while soft wheat has less protein. Protein contains the gluten that allows breads and baked goods to rise. Though there are many types of flours to use for baking, I will only call for three in this cookbook: all-purpose flour, whole wheat flour, and cake flour. Unless specified as cake flour or whole wheat flour, when "flour" is listed in ingredients, I am referring to all-purpose flour.

WHOLE WHEAT FLOUR—This type of flour is made by mashing the whole grain of wheat, also known as the wheat berry. All of the grain (bran, germ, and endosperm) is used and nothing is lost in the process of making the flour. Whole wheat flour contains vitamins, minerals, and protein. It is used in baking breads and other baked goods, and is also commonly mixed with other lighter white flours.

ALL-PURPOSE FLOUR—This is the most commonly used type of flour in baked goods. It has a good balance of hard and soft wheat, and comes bleached or unbleached. I use unbleached all-purpose flour for recipes in this book that call for flour. It is widely used in cookies, cakes, muffins, quick breads, biscuits, and crusts.

CAKE FLOUR—Cake flour is a fine-textured, soft-wheat flour with a high starch content. It has the lowest protein content of any wheat flour and has about 8–10 percent gluten. It is chlorinated (a bleaching process which leaves the flour slightly acidic and distributes fat more evenly through the batter to improve texture). This flour is excellent for baking light cakes with greater volume, and is used in some quick breads, muffins, and cookies to give them a melt-in-your-mouth texture.

VANILLA—I am a huge fan of vanilla. I always use pure vanilla extract or madagascar bourbon pure vanilla extract. I do not recommend ever using imitation vanilla. It does not have a true vanilla taste—not even close. My favorite brand is Nielsen-Massey, but you can use any good-quality brand you can find.

VANILLA BEAN PASTE—Nielsen-Massey also makes an amazing Madagascar Bourbon Pure Vanilla Bean Paste. It's a combination of their Madagascar Bourbon Pure Vanilla Extract and real seeds from the vanilla pod. It's a thick consistency, similar to molasses, and is great for flavoring batters you don't want to thin. If you love having black specks of vanilla beans in your recipes and love a great vanilla flavor, this is it!

EGGS—This cookbook calls for lots and lots of eggs. You may use organic, free-range eggs for any recipe calling for eggs, or use whatever you have on hand. Just make sure you use the largest, freshest eggs that are available to you. Always use eggs at room temperature so they will whip up nice and fluffy.

SUGAR—Recipes in this book calling for sugar refer to granulated sugar unless otherwise indicated. Granulated sugar is highly refined cane or beet sugar and is white with a fine grain texture. It is the most widely used sugar in baking.

CONFECTIONERS' SUGAR—Also known as powdered sugar or icing sugar, confectioners' sugar is granulated sugar that has been crushed into a fine powder with a small amount of cornstarch to prevent clumping. It dissolves very quickly and is great for making icings. It can also be used for dusting desserts to make them tasty and attractive, giving them a with a white powdery finish.

LIGHT BROWN SUGAR—When a recipe calls for brown sugar, it implies light brown sugar that is "packed" when measuring. When packing brown sugar into a measuring cup, take the back of the spoon and press down as far you can. Continue to fill the measuring cup using this method. Brown sugar is white sugar that contains molasses. It has a richer, more distinct taste. There is a difference between light and dark brown sugar, but for this book, I will only use light brown sugar.

MILK—I use whole milk in all my baking recipes unless otherwise indicated. The extra fat in whole milk adds more moistness to baked goods than lower fat versions, making them taste even better.

BUTTERMILK—I can't say enough about buttermilk, especially how brilliant it makes pancakes taste. Buttermilk tastes like sour cream and butter combined. It has great a tangy and buttery flavor and adds moistness and a lighter texture to cakes, muffins, breads, and pancakes.

HALF-AND-HALF—This is equal parts light cream and milk. It is slightly creamier than whole milk, and gives a more tender crumb to baked goods than whole milk will.

LIQUID COFFEE CREAMER—Coffee creamer is a flavored non-dairy creamer typically used to add flavor to coffee. I use coffee creamers to add moisture and flavor to icings, cakes, breads, muffins, and pancakes. Do not use powdered coffee creamers to substitute for liquid coffee creamers when making the recipes in this book.

UNSALTED BUTTER—Otherwise known as "sweet cream butter" or "unsalted sweet cream butter." When purchasing butter, always read the label and make sure it's USDA AA butter. Using unsalted butter is simply a way of controlling your salt intake. If you are using salted butter in place of unsalted butter, omit the added salt called for in the recipe.

SEA SALT—Sea salt has a different taste and more noticeable texture than ordinary table salt. For that reason, I only use sea salt for topping cupcakes, bread puddings, or other desserts so that the texture and flavor of the salt comes through in each bite.

RAPID RISE YEAST—This is a time-saving product that has the same functions as active dry yeast, but does not need to be dissolved in water before adding it to dry ingredients. It also doesn't need the extra rising time before baking that active dry yeast does, which is a great time saver.

GOOD MORNING MUFFINS

These fresh, made-from-scratch muffins will be devoured straight from the oven. There is just nothing better.

Every time I make delicious blueberry muffins, I think of summer. Every bite is bursting with plump, juicy blueberries and bright yellow lemon zest. It takes me back to when I was a child, picking blueberries in my Grandmother's yard on a warm, sunny day.

BLUEBERRY LEMON MUFFINS

makes 24 small muffins

3 cups flour

¾ cup sugar

1½ Tbsp. baking powder

3 eggs

1½ cups buttermilk

6 Tbsp. butter,
  melted and cooled

2 tsp. pure vanilla extract

zest and juice of 1 lemon

1 pint fresh blueberries, rinsed

confectioners' sugar for topping

1 Preheat oven to 400 degrees. Line cupcake pan with cupcake liners. In a large bowl, sift flour, sugar, and baking powder together and create a well in the center. Set aside. In a separate bowl, whisk together eggs, buttermilk, melted butter, vanilla, and lemon juice until light and fluffy, about 2 minutes. Fold wet mixture into dry mixture until just combined. Fold in lemon zest and blueberries very gently. Do not overmix. Using a large cookie scoop, add batter to each liner (or use a ¼ measuring cup).

2 Bake for 8 minutes at 400 degrees. Lower temperature to 325 degrees and bake for another 10 minutes or until lightly golden brown and firm to the touch. Cool slightly on wire racks and sprinkle with confectioners' sugar before serving if desired.

The warm days of summer are perfect for baking up a batch of these sunny little fellas. I bake them in a standard cupcake pan, since they are sweet and tart. Enjoy them bright and early in the morning, and don't forget to top them with luscious sweetened coconut for a tropical touch and added flavor.

LEMON COCONUT MUFFINS

makes 24 small muffins

3 cups flour

1 cup sugar

1 tsp. baking soda

1½ tsp. cream of tartar

½ tsp. salt

2 large eggs

1¼ cups milk

½ cup butter, melted

zest and juice of 1 lemon

1 tsp. lemon extract

shredded, sweetened coconut

1 Preheat oven to 400 degrees and prepare a cupcake pan with cupcake liners. Whisk together flour, sugar, baking soda, cream of tartar, and salt in a large bowl. Create a well in the center of the flour mixture and set aside. In a separate bowl, whisk together eggs, milk, melted butter, lemon zest, lemon juice and extract until fluffy, about 2 minutes. Stir wet ingredients into dry ingredients until just moistened. Do not overmix.

2 Using a large cookie scoop, add batter to greased cupcake pan, about two-thirds full. Bake for 6 minutes at 400 degrees. Lower heat to 325 degrees and bake for another 12 minutes, or until they are lightly golden brown and the center is firm to the touch. Sprinkle with shredded coconut before serving.

These glorious muffins have loads of fresh, sweet strawberries in every bite. I bake them in cupcake pans instead of muffin pans because I like to top them with whipped cream and treat them like a tiny dessert.

FARM FRESH STRAWBERRY MUFFINS

makes 12 muffins

2 cups flour

½ cup sugar

½ tsp. salt

1 Tbsp. baking powder

3 cups diced strawberries

1 cup milk

¼ cup vegetable oil

2 eggs

1 tsp. vanilla extract

frozen whipped topping

1 Preheat oven to 400 degrees. Line a standard cupcake pan with cupcake liners. In a large bowl, sift all dry ingredients. Add strawberries and toss to coat. In a large bowl fitted to an electric mixer beat milk, vegetable oil, eggs, and vanilla extract for 2 minutes. Add wet mixture to dry mixture and stir only until combined. Bits of flour will still be visible. Do not overmix.

2 With a large cookie scoop (or ¼ cup) fill each cupcake liner with batter, ensuring there are chunks of strawberries in each cup. Bake for 6 minutes at 400 degrees. Lower temperature to 375 degrees and bake for another 15 minutes or until muffins are lightly golden brown and firm to the touch. Serve at room temperature with a dollop of whipped topping or sprinkled with confectioners' sugar.

My kids love anything with chocolate chips in them, so this muffin recipe is a favorite at my house. The kids love to eat them warm so the chocolate chips are gooey. They taste great with a frosty glass of chocolate milk.

PEANUT BUTTER CHOCOLATE CHIP MUFFINS

makes 8 muffins

2¼ cups flour

2 tsp. baking powder

½ tsp. salt

1 cup brown sugar

6 Tbsp. butter, melted and cooled

½ cup smooth peanut butter

2 eggs

1 cup milk

1 cup semi-sweet mini chocolate chips

1 Preheat oven to 375 degrees. Spray a muffin pan with baking spray or add muffin liners. In a large bowl, whisk together flour, baking powder, salt, and brown sugar.

2 In a medium bowl, whisk together melted butter, peanut butter, eggs, and milk until smooth. Pour into flour mixture and stir until just combined. Stir in chocolate chips. Batter will be thick.

3 Using a large cookie scoop, add two scoops of batter to each muffin cup. If not using a large cookie scoop, be sure to fill each muffin cup to the top so you get a tall crown.

4 Bake for 18–20 minutes, until tops of muffins are firm. Cool slightly on a wire rack and serve warm.

There isn't a scent quite so pleasant as Sugar and Spice Gingerbread Muffins. I love baking them in the fall when the leaves are colorful and pumpkins are on the porch. These muffins spread warmth and comfort in our household, and the spicy sweet smell lasts for hours. I love to dunk my gingerbread muffins in hot ginger tea, and the kids enjoy theirs with apple juice.

SUGAR AND SPICE GINGERBREAD MUFFINS

makes 8 muffins

¼ cup brown sugar

½ cup molasses

⅓ cup milk

⅓ cup unsweetened applesauce

1 egg

2 cups flour

1 tsp. baking powder

1 tsp. ground ginger

½ tsp. salt

½ tsp. baking soda

1 tsp. ground cinnamon

½ tsp. ground allspice

2 Tbsp. butter, melted

sugar for sprinkling

1 Heat oven to 400 degrees. Line standard muffin pan with paper liners. In medium bowl, whisk brown sugar, molasses, milk, unsweetened applesauce, and egg with a wire whisk. In a large bowl, sift all dry ingredients. Add wet ingredients and stir until combined.

2 Using a large cookie scoop, add two scoops of batter to prepared muffin cups. Batter should reach the top of pan. Bake at 400 degrees for 8 minutes. Lower oven temperature to 375 degrees and bake for another 15-20 minutes, or until muffins are lightly golden brown and spring back when touched in the middle. When done baking, remove pan from oven and let muffins sit for 5 minutes in pan. Remove muffins from pan and let cool on wire cookie rack. Spread melted butter on top and sprinkle with sugar.

When I tasted these muffins, they quickly became one of my favorites. The combination of raspberries, blueberries, and blackberries gives it remarkable flavor. The banana chunks add moistness, texture, and a wonderful sweetness that complements the cinnamon streusel topping.

TRIPLE BERRY BANANA CHUNK MUFFINS WITH OAT STREUSEL TOPPING

makes 8 muffins

3½ cups flour

4 tsp. baking powder

½ tsp. salt

1⅓ cups sugar

10 Tbsp. butter, melted and cooled slightly

1 cup milk

1 cup sour cream

2 eggs

1½ tsp. vanilla extract

1½ cups chopped mixed berries, fresh or frozen

1 Tbsp. lemon zest or zest of one lemon

1 banana, sliced and quartered

STREUSEL TOPPING

¼ cup flour

¼ cup oats

¼ cup brown sugar

1 tsp. cinnamon

4 Tbsp. butter, softened

1 Preheat oven to 400 degrees. Spray muffin pan with baking spray or line with muffin liners. In a large mixing bowl, sift together flour, baking powder, and salt and mix well. In a medium mixing bowl, whisk together sugar, butter, milk, sour cream, eggs, and vanilla until well combined.

2 Add wet ingredients to dry ingredients and fold gently with a rubber spatula until mixture is moist. Add in berries, lemon zest, and bananas. Continue to fold ingredients together until just moistened. Do not overmix. Batter will be lumpy. Using a large cookie scoop, add two scoops of batter into prepared muffin cups. The batter should come up to the top of the muffin pan. Mix streusel topping ingredients in a small bowl, using two forks or a pastry cutter until mixture is combined and looks like coarse crumbs. Apply 1 tablespoon mixture to each muffin. Bake at 400 degrees for 8 minutes. Lower oven temperature to 325 degrees and bake for another 20 minutes, or until muffins are lightly golden brown and spring back when touched in the middle. When done baking, remove pan from oven and let muffins sit for 5 minutes. Remove muffins from pan and let cool on wire cookie rack.

I created this muffin to mimic my favorite holiday recipe, cranberry nut bread. It's a lovely scented muffin bursting with tart fresh cranberries and sweet orange zest. The almonds add a nice crunchy topping, and the confectioners' sugar cuts down on the tartness of the cranberries while complementing their flavor.

CRANBERRY ALMOND MUFFINS

makes 8 muffins

3½ cups flour

4 tsp. baking powder

½ tsp. baking soda

1 tsp. salt

1⅓ cups sugar

10 Tbsp. butter, melted and cooled slightly

1 cup milk

1 cup sour cream

2 eggs

1 tsp. pure orange extract

1 tsp. pure almond extract

1½ cups chopped fresh or frozen cranberries

2 Tbsp. finely grated orange zest

½ cup sliced almonds

confectioners' sugar for dusting

1 Preheat oven to 400 degrees. Line muffin pan with muffin liners. In a large mixing bowl, sift together flour, baking powder, baking soda, and salt. In a medium mixing bowl, whisk together sugar, butter, milk, sour cream, eggs, and extracts until well combined. Pour wet ingredients into dry ingredients and fold gently with a rubber spatula until barely moistened. Fold in cranberries and orange zest until just combined. Lumps of flour should still be visible.

2 Using a large cookie scoop, add two scoops of batter to prepared muffin cups. Batter should reach top of pan. Top each muffin with 1 tablespoon sliced almonds. Bake at 400 degrees for 8 minutes. Lower oven temperature to 325 degrees and bake for another 20 minutes, or until muffins are lightly golden brown and spring back when touched. When done baking, remove pan from oven and let muffins sit for 5 minutes in pan. Remove muffins from pan and let cool on wire cookie rack. Dust with sugar before serving.

Rich, dark, and fudgy is the best way to describe these double chocolate muffins. They are super indulgent and absolutely must be paired with a frosty glass of ice cold milk. You'll be smitten when you try these.

DOUBLE CHOCOLATE MUFFINS

makes 6 muffins

2 cups flour

1 cup cocoa powder

¾ cup sugar

1 Tbsp. baking powder

½ tsp. salt

1 cup semi-sweet chocolate chips, plus ⅓ cup for sprinkling

2 eggs

1¼ cups milk

1¼ tsp. vanilla extract

⅓ cup vegetable oil

2 Tbsp. butter, melted

1 Preheat oven to 400 degrees. Spray a muffin tin with baking spray with flour. In a large bowl, mix the flour, cocoa powder, sugar, baking powder, salt, and chocolate chips. In another bowl, whisk eggs until light and fluffy. Add milk, vanilla, oil, and melted butter and mix until combined. Add the wet ingredients to the dry ingredients and mix until just combined. Batter will be lumpy. Do not overmix. Using a large cookie scoop, fill muffin tin with batter about ¾ full. Sprinkle the remaining chocolate chips on tops of muffins.

2 Bake at 400 degrees for 8 minutes. Lower heat to 350 degrees and bake for 22 minutes, or until a toothpick inserted into the center of a muffin comes out clean. Remove pan from the oven and let muffins cool for five minutes. Remove muffins from pan and let them cool another five minutes on a wire rack.

Caramel apples remind me of fall, when the kids are back in school and hayrides, pumpkin carving, and trick-or-treating are right around the corner. These muffins are moist and sweet with chunks of apples and cinnamon in every bite. The caramel topping adds a classic caramel apple flavor that makes them over-the-top delicious.

CARAMEL APPLE CHUNK MUFFINS

makes 8 muffins

3½ cups flour

4 tsp. baking powder

½ tsp. baking soda

1 tsp. cinnamon

1½ cup chopped apples
   (I use Granny Smith)

1⅓ cup sugar

10 Tbsp. butter, melted

1 cup milk

1 cup unsweetened applesauce

2 eggs

1 jar caramel ice cream topping

2 Tbsp. cinnamon

2 Tbsp. sugar

1 Preheat oven to 400 degrees. Spray muffin pan with baking spray. In a large bowl, add dry ingredients and whisk together until combined. Toss apples with flour mixture to coat. In a medium bowl, combine the next five ingredients with a wire whisk until well combined. Add wet mixture to dry mixture and mix just until moistened. Lumps of flour will still appear. Do not overmix. In a small bowl, combine cinnamon and sugar to sprinkle on muffins tops.

2 With a large cookie scoop, add 2 scoops of batter to each muffin cup. Batter should reach the top of the pan. Sprinkle each muffin generously with cinnamon and sugar mixture. Bake at 400 degrees for 8 minutes. Lower heat to 375 degrees and bake for another 20 minutes, or until centers of muffins spring back when touched. Remove muffins from pan onto wire cookie wrack. Once cooled, drizzle with caramel topping and serve immediately.

I once read that rosemary improves focus. So as an experiment, I planted rosemary seeds, and in no time I had a huge rosemary bush that smelled delicious. I began using it in many recipes, including these tasty pumpkin muffins. While I am not certain it helped to improve focus, it certainly went down in the books as the best pumpkin muffin recipe ever tasted in our house. The rosemary went surprisingly well with pumpkin and all the other wonderful spices.

PUMPKIN ROSEMARY MUFFINS

makes 6 muffins

2 cups flour

1 tsp. baking soda

½ tsp. salt

2 tsp. pumpkin pie spice

½ tsp. nutmeg

¾ cup sugar

¾ cup brown sugar

½ cup vegetable oil

1 cup water

½ cup applesauce

½ cup canned puréed pumpkin, (not pumpkin pie filling)

2 eggs

1 tsp. vanilla extract

4 Tbsp. finely chopped fresh rosemary

1 Preheat oven to 400 degrees. Line muffin tin with muffin liners. In a large bowl, whisk together flour, baking soda, salt, pumpkin pie spice, and nutmeg. Set aside. In a mixing bowl, combine sugars, oil, water, applesauce, pumpkin, eggs, and vanilla and mix on low speed until completely combined. Stir in rosemary. Add wet ingredients to dry ingredients and stir until just combined.

2 Using a large cookie scoop, add two scoops of batter to prepared muffin pan. Batter should reach top of pan. Bake at 400 degrees for 10 minutes. Lower oven temperature to 325 degrees and bake for another 20 minutes, or until muffins are lightly golden brown and spring back when touched in the middle. When done baking, remove pan from oven and let muffins sit for 5 minutes in pan. Remove muffins from pan and let cool on wire cookie rack.

Bananas, buttermilk, pecans, cinnamon…what's not to love about these Banana Nut Muffins? It's an intensely moist muffin with strong banana flavor, with the extra sweet, nutty goodness of chopped pecans. Adding cinnamon gives them a subtle hint of spice, while the buttermilk provides a creamy tang that makes these muffins moist and delicious.

BANANA NUT MUFFINS

makes 6–8 muffins

2½ cups flour

1 cup sugar

1 tsp. baking soda

1 tsp. baking powder

¼ tsp. salt

1 tsp. cinnamon

½ cup chopped pecans

3 ripe bananas

½ cup vegetable oil

2 eggs

½ cup buttermilk

2 Using a large cookie scoop, add two scoops of batter to prepared muffin cups. Batter should reach top of pan. Bake at 400 degrees for 10 minutes. Lower oven temperature to 325 degrees and bake for another 23 minutes, or until muffins are lightly golden brown and spring back when touched in the middle. When done baking, remove pan from oven and let muffins sit for 5 minutes in pan. Remove muffins from pan and let cool on wire cookie rack. Serve warm or at room temperature.

1 Preheat oven to 400 degrees. Line a muffin tin with muffin liners. In a large bowl, sift dry ingredients together. Mix in pecans and make a well in the center. In a separate bowl, with an electric mixer on low speed, add bananas and beat until mashed, leaving small lumps. Add remaining wet ingredients and mix until combined. Add wet mixture to dry mixture. Fold together with a spoon just until moistened.

COME ON OVER
COFFEE CAKES

Invite your neighbors over for a slice of heaven with one of these moist and fruity coffee cakes that are sure to please a crowd.

I love cakes that are so moist and flavorful that they don't need icing. This cakes fits the bill. Since my daughter has tree nut allergies, I bake this cake without walnuts. But adding walnuts to this refreshing, sweet, and aromatic cake would make it even more blissful.

CRANBERRY SNACK CAKE

serves 8–10

CROWELL

4 eggs

2 cups sugar

1 cup butter, slightly softened and cut into chunks

zest of 1 orange

1 Tbsp. vanilla extract

1 tsp. salt

4 tsp. buttermilk

2 cups flour

1 (12-oz.) bag fresh cranberries

1 cup walnuts, chopped (optional)

1 Preheat oven to 350 degrees. Grease and flour a 10-inch round cake pan or use baking spray with flour. In a large bowl, beat eggs and sugar for 5–7 minutes, until eggs have increased in volume. Add butter, orange zest, and vanilla and beat until incorporated, about 2 minutes. Beat in salt and buttermilk.

2 Stir in flour until just combined, and fold in cranberries. Scrape batter into prepared pan. Bake on middle rack in a preheated oven for 1 hour. Center may still be a tad under baked (doesn't spring back when touched), but will continue baking while cooling on a wire rack. Do not remove cake from pan while cooling. Once cooled completely, about an hour or so, remove from pan and place on a cake stand. Dust with confectioners' sugar before slicing.

This cake may not be a traditional breakfast staple, but if coffee cake, pastries, and muffins are acceptable for breakfast, this is too. It's such a pretty cake to display on a holiday buffet table, or at a brunch you are hosting when you really want to wow your guests. It doesn't need sugar or frosting. The pineapples and cherries are sweet enough on their own.

CLASSIC PINEAPPLE UPSIDE-DOWN CAKE

serves 12

1 stick butter

¾ cup brown sugar

12 canned pineapple rings in juice

2 cups flour

2 tsp. baking powder

¼ tsp. salt

¼ tsp. ground nutmeg

1 tsp. cinnamon

½ cup butter, softened

½ cup sugar

½ cup brown sugar

3 eggs

½ cup milk

1 tsp. vanilla

12 maraschino cherries

1 Heat oven to 350 degrees. Butter the bottom and sides of a 9 × 13 baking pan. Line bottom of pan with parchment paper; set pan aside.

2 Melt 1 stick of butter in a medium saucepan over low heat. Stir in ¾ cup brown sugar. Bring to a boil over medium heat, stirring constantly. Pour into prepared pan. Drain pineapple rings, reserving ½ cup juice. Place 10–12 rings in bottom of pan.

3 In a medium bowl, whisk together flour, baking powder, salt, nutmeg, and cinnamon. In a mixing bowl, beat 1 stick softened butter, sugar, and ½ cup brown sugar on medium speed for 2 minutes, scraping sides of bowl occasionally. Add eggs one at a time until combined. On low speed, beat in half of flour mixture. Add reserved ½ cup pineapple juice and milk and beat until combined. Beat in remaining flour mixture and vanilla.

4 Gently spread batter evenly over top of pineapple slices in pan. Bake 35–40 minutes, or until a toothpick inserted near center comes out clean. Cool in pan on wire rack 10 minutes. Do not invert cake before this or pineapple may stick to pan. Place a baking sheet over coffee cake and carefully invert. If any pineapple sticks to pan, gently replace on cake top. Serve warm, topped with maraschino cherries. Store at room temperature up to 3 days.

This is one of my favorite coffee cakes, because to me the combination of apricots and almonds is a marriage made in heaven. The filling is sweet and tangy and is tucked inside a flavorful cake. Serve this coffee cake at a holiday brunch or as a special Sunday treat. It's so delicious, you have to share it.

ALMOND APRICOT JAM COFFEE CAKE

serves 8–10

FILLING

¾ cup sliced almonds
¼ cup brown sugar
¼ cup apricot jam
½ tsp. ground cinnamon

COFFEE CAKE

2 cups flour
1 tsp. baking powder
1 tsp. baking soda
1 cup butter, softened
½ cup sugar
1 cup brown sugar
3 eggs
1 cup sour cream
1 tsp. vanilla
1 tsp. almond extract

GLAZE

½ cup confectioners' sugar
1 tsp. milk
½ tsp. almond extract

1 Heat oven to 350 degrees. Grease and flour a 12-cup fluted tube cake pan or Bundt pan. In small bowl, mix all filling ingredients until well blended.

2 In medium bowl, mix flour, baking powder, and baking soda. In large bowl, beat butter and sugars on medium speed, scraping bowl occasionally until fluffy. Beat in eggs, one at a time. Beat in sour cream, vanilla, and almond extract until blended. Gradually beat in flour mixture until blended. Spoon 3 cups batter into pan. Spoon filling over batter to within ½ inch of edge. Spoon remaining batter over filling. Bake 30–35 minutes, or until toothpick inserted in center comes out clean. Cool 15 minutes, and then remove from pan to cooling rack. Cool to room temperature.

3 In small bowl, mix all glaze ingredients until smooth and thin enough to drizzle. Stir in additional milk, ½ teaspoon at a time, if necessary. Drizzle glaze over coffee cake.

Buckles are a single layer cake with berries added to the batter, baked with a sweet streusel topping. Its a favorite in the South for brunch, and since this recipe makes a lot, it's great to take to a church social or potluck holiday gathering. Drizzling melted white chocolate on top makes the raspberries taste spectacular.

RASPBERRY WHITE CHOCOLATE BUCKLE

serves 12–16

CAKE

2 cups flour

2½ tsp. baking powder

¼ tsp. salt

½ cup shortening

1 cup sugar

2 eggs

½ cup milk

2 cups frozen or fresh raspberries

TOPPING

½ cup flour

½ cup sugar

1 tsp. cinnamon

¼ cup butter

1 cup white chocolate chips

1 Preheat oven to 350 degrees. Grease an 8 × 8 baking dish and set aside. In a medium bowl, combine flour, baking powder, and salt and set aside.

2 In a large bowl, beat shortening with mixer on medium speed for 20 seconds. Add sugar. Beat on medium to high speed until light and fluffy. Add eggs and beat well. Alternately add flour mixture and milk, starting with flour mixture, to beaten egg mixture. Beat on low until smooth after each addition.

3 Spoon batter into prepared pan. Sprinkle with raspberries. In a small bowl, combine topping ingredients using a pastry blender, until mixture resembles coarse crumbs. Sprinkle over raspberries. Bake for 50 minutes or until golden brown.

4 Melt white chocolate chips in microwave at 20 second intervals until melted, stirring after each interval. Once completely melted and lump free, drizzle over top of baked and cooled raspberry buckle. Serve at room temperature.

I bake this delicious coffee cake for a special breakfast treat when we have overnight guests. It's simple to put together and it's always gone in minutes. The cake flour adds a tender, melt-in-your-mouth crumb, while the sour cream makes the cake super moist. I love the cinnamon brown sugar layer in the middle. But then again, I'm a sucker for anything with sugar and cinnamon.

CLASSIC CINNAMON COFFEE CAKE

serves 16

FILLING

½ cup brown sugar

1½ tsp. cinnamon

COFFEE CAKE

2 cups flour

1 cup cake flour

1½ tsp. baking powder

1½ tsp. baking soda

½ tsp. salt

1½ cups sugar

1½ sticks butter, softened

1½ tsp. vanilla

3 eggs

1½ cups sour cream

GLAZE

2 cups confectioners' sugar

1 tsp. vanilla

2-3 Tbsp. milk

1 Heat oven to 350 degrees. Grease 12-cup bundt pan. In small bowl, mix filling ingredients and set aside. In medium bowl, sift flours, baking powder, baking soda, and salt and set aside. In large bowl, beat sugar, butter, vanilla, and eggs with electric mixer on medium speed for 2 minutes, scraping bowl occasionally. On low speed, beat in half of flour mixture until just combined. Add sour cream and beat until combined. Add remaining flour mixture and beat until just combined.

2 Spread ⅓ batter (about 2 cups) in pan; sprinkle with ⅓ filling (about 6 tablespoons). Spread remaining batter and then top with remaining filling. Bake about 45 minutes, or until a toothpick inserted near center comes out clean. Cool 10 minutes. Remove from pan to wire rack and cool to room temperature.

3 Meanwhile, make glaze by stirring together confectioners' sugar, vanilla, and milk. Drizzle glaze onto cake and serve.

This recipe has been a staple in my home for 15 years. I usually make it in the summer, because that's when blueberries are at their peak in Virginia. This buckle is packed with warm blueberries bursting in a delicate, lemon-scented cake with a sugary oat streusel topping. Start your morning with a huge slice and a cup of hot tea, and I do believe all will go right with your day.

BLUEBERRY BUCKLE

serves 6–8

STREUSEL

½ cup flour

⅓ cup brown sugar

2 Tbsp. sugar

1 tsp. cinnamon

½ tsp. salt

4 Tbsp. butter, cut into 8 pieces and softened

CAKE

2 cups flour

2 tsp. baking powder

1½ sticks butter, softened

¾ cup sugar

1 tsp. lemon zest

juice of half a lemon

2 tsp. vanilla extract

3 eggs

2 cups blueberries

1 For the streusel: Using an electric mixer fitted with paddle attachment, combine flour, brown sugar, sugar, cinnamon, and salt on low speed until well combined and no large brown sugar clumps remain. Add butter. Beat on low speed until mixture has no large butter pieces, about 2 minutes. Transfer to bowl and set aside.

2 For the cake: Preheat oven to 350 degrees and spray an 8-inch round cake pan with baking spray. Sift flour and baking powder together in bowl and set aside. Using stand mixer fitted with paddle, beat butter, sugar, lemon zest, and lemon juice on medium-high speed until light and fluffy, about 3 minutes, scraping bowl as necessary. Beat in vanilla until combined. With mixer on medium speed, add eggs 1 at a time. Scrape the bowl and continue to beat until fully incorporated. With mixer on low speed, gradually add flour mixture. Beat until flour is almost fully incorporated, about 30 seconds. Stir batter with rubber spatula, scraping bowl, until no flour remaining. Batter will be very heavy and thick. Gently fold in blueberries.

3 Pour batter to prepared pan. Spread batter evenly to pan edges and smooth surface. Sprinkle streusel evenly over batter. Bake until cake is deep golden brown and toothpick comes out clean, about 45 minutes. Transfer to wire rack and let cool.

This is one of my husband's favorite southern recipes. Every time we go out to eat for breakfast, he orders biscuits and gravy. Adding apple to the gravy gives it a pleasing new flavor that pairs well with the pork sausage. Bake a double batch of the biscuits to serve later with dinner. They are flaky, buttery, and simply amazing.

JOHN'S BUTTERMILK BISCUITS AND APPLE SAUSAGE GRAVY

10–12 servings

FOR BISCUITS

2 cups flour

2 tsp. sugar

2½ tsp. baking powder

½ tsp. baking soda

½ tsp. salt

4 Tbsp. butter, chilled, sliced, and cut into fourths

1 cup buttermilk

FOR APPLE SAUSAGE GRAVY

2 tsp. butter

1 medium apple, cored and diced (about 1¼ cups)

1 lb. pork sausage

3 Tbsp. flour

2¼ cups milk

½ cup diced yellow onion

½ tsp. dried onion

⅛ tsp. coarse ground black pepper

dash of cayenne pepper

1 Preheat oven to 400 degrees. Lightly spray cookie sheet with nonstick spray. For biscuits; Add flour, sugar, baking powder, baking soda, and salt in a medium mixing bowl and whisk to combine. Cut in chilled butter using a pastry blender, until butter looks like fine crumbs. Stir in buttermilk with a wooden spoon until dough is mixed together and is a little sticky. Turn dough out onto a floured surface and knead lightly, until dough comes together and becomes more elastic. Do not overwork dough. Roll dough into a 9 × 5 rectangle (½ inch thick). Dust the top of the dough lightly with flour. Fold dough in half and reroll to another 9 × 5 rectangle. Cut dough with a 1¾-inch biscuit cutter to form 12 dough rounds. Gather scraps and gently pat the dough together again to cut more biscuits if needed.

2 Place biscuit rounds 1 inch apart on prepared baking sheet. Bake 12 minutes, or until biscuits are golden. Set aside baked biscuits.

3 For gravy: In a 10-inch nonstick skillet, melt butter over medium heat. Add diced apple and cook 4–7 minutes, stirring occasionally, until tender. Remove, cover, and keep warm.

4 Increase heat to medium high. In same skillet, add sausage and diced onions and cook for 5 minutes, stirring frequently, until no longer pink. Add flour, stirring constantly until brown. Stir in milk with wire whisk. Cook about 3 minutes, stirring constantly, until mixture thickens. Stir in apple, dried onion, black pepper, and cayenne. Pour hot gravy over fresh baked biscuits and enjoy.

BAKER'S TIP

Always keep a light hand when working with dough. Overworking it will result in a tough and dry biscuit.

The key to light and fluffy scones is to start with cold ingredients and work the dough ever so gently and as little as possible. After they are baked and cooled, dust them with confectioners' sugar and drizzle with your favorite warmed jam or a smear of butter.

CREAM SCONES WITH RASPBERRY SAUCE

serves 6

¾ cup heavy cream, chilled

1 egg

2 cups flour

¼ cup sugar, plus more for sprinkling

2 tsp. baking powder

6 Tbsp. cold butter, cut into small pieces

4 Tbsp. butter, melted

½ cup raspberry jam

confectioners' sugar for dusting

1 Preheat oven to 400 degrees. Whisk together cream and egg. In a large bowl, whisk together flour, sugar, and baking powder. With a pastry blender, cut butter into flour mixture until crumbly. With a fork, stir in cream mixture until just combined. Do not overwork dough.

2 Turn out dough to a lightly floured work surface and pat into a 6-inch circle. Cut into 6 wedges and transfer separately to a parchment-lined round cookie sheet. Brush tops with melted butter and sprinkle with granulated sugar. Bake until golden, 16–18 minutes, rotating sheet halfway through.

3 In a small bowl, microwave raspberry jam for 30 seconds or until thin and completely warmed. Stir jam and with a spoon, drizzle it onto each baked scone. Dust with confectioners' sugar if desired.

The kids love these sweet little homemade breakfast treats, especially when I use buttermilk. It gives each donut a buttery, melt-in-your-mouth texture that tastes delicious and makes them truly addictive. The best part is that these donuts are baked, not fried. If you have donut lovers in your house, you might want to make a double batch. These will go quickly.

CINNAMON BUTTERMILK DONUTS

makes 6 donuts

1 cup flour

2 Tbsp. cornstarch

1 tsp. baking powder

⅓ cup sugar

¾ cup buttermilk

1 Tbsp. butter, melted

1½ tsp. vinegar

1 egg, lightly beaten

CINNAMON SUGAR TOPPING

¼ cup sugar

1 Tbsp. ground cinnamon

2 Tbsp. melted butter

1 Preheat oven to 425 degrees. Spray a 6-cavity donut pan with baking spray. If using a 12-cavity donut pan, double recipe. In a medium bowl, sift together flour, cornstarch, baking powder, salt, and sugar.

2 In a small bowl mix together buttermilk, melted butter, vinegar, and egg. Pour the egg mixture into center of dry mixture. Mix until just combined. Using a large cookie scoop, transfer batter to each donut cavity and jiggle pan so the dough falls into cavity and off of the center peak. Bake for 7–8 minutes. Remove from oven and let rest in pan for 2 minutes. Meanwhile, combine sugar and cinnamon in a small bowl. With a pastry brush, apply melted butter to the top of each baked donut and dredge in cinnamon/sugar mixture. Serve warm or at room temperature.

This is the mother of all banana bread recipes. I will never make another banana bread recipe again without using spiced rum. It really adds depth of flavor and brings out the banana more than I ever anticipated. I am truly in love with this recipe, and I know you will be too.

SPICED RUM BANANA BREAD

makes 2 loaves

2 eggs

5 ripe bananas, mashed

2 Tbsp. Captain Morgan spiced rum
    or 1 Tbsp. rum extract

1 cup sugar

½ cup vegetable oil

2 cups flour

1½ tsp. baking powder

½ tsp. baking soda

¼ tsp. ground cinnamon

¼ cup chopped pecans

1 cup sweetened shredded coconut

1 Preheat oven to 375 degrees. Grease two standard loaf pans. Set aside. In a medium bowl, beat two eggs with a wire whisk. Add bananas, rum, sugar, and oil and mix together until combined.

2 In a separate large bowl, whisk together flour, baking powder, baking soda, and cinnamon. Make a well in center of flour mixture. Add entire egg mixture to center of flour mixture and mix until just combined. Fold in pecans and coconut. Pour batter into prepared pans. Bake for 30 minutes or until lightly golden brown and middle is just barely set. Remove pans from oven and cool on a wire rack for 15 minutes. Remove loaves from pans and cool until room temperature.

I absolutely love food that is sweet and spicy at the same time. The complex flavors of sweet baked apples, cranberries, and apricot jam mixed with jalapeños gives this pastry dynamite flavor. Melted Brie brings it down a notch and adds even more depth. All of this goodness is wrapped in a flaky ready-made pizza dough, which is a huge time saver.

SPICY APRICOT SAUSAGE PASTRY

serves 6–8

1 lb. pork sausage

1 can refrigerated pizza crust

1 jar apricot jam or preserves

1 small granny smith apple, cored
   and sliced ⅛-inch thick

1 jalapeño, finely chopped

8 oz. Brie cheese, cut in ¼-inch cubes

5 Tbsp. sweetened dried cranberries

1 Heat oven to 375 degrees. Line 15 × 10 nonstick pan with parchment paper. Spray parchment paper with cooking spray. In a large skillet, cook sausage over medium-high heat 10–15 minutes, stirring frequently, until sausage is no longer pink. Drain.

2 On a cookie sheet, unroll dough. Press dough almost to edges of cookie sheet. In a small saucepan on medium-high heat, combine jam and jalapeño. Stir until a thin consistency, about 2–3 minutes. Spread mixture down the middle of the dough, leaving about a 1 inch seam in diameter. Top with apple slices, cheese cubes, sausage, and cranberries.

3 Using kitchen scissors or sharp knife, make cuts 2 inches apart on long sides of the dough to within ¼ inch of filling. Fold strips of dough diagonally over filling, alternating from side to side, carefully stretching dough as needed. Bake 20–25 minutes, or until dough is lightly golden brown and filling is bubbling. Can be served warm or at room temperature. Store in refrigerator.

I made these danishes huge and cut them into fourths. The recipe made four large danishes, so as you can see, you could feed a small crowd with one recipe. They were light and fluffy, with terrific sweet yeast dough taste that smells like heaven while baking. Top with any flavor fruit filling you like best. I love cherries and went with that.

JUMBO CHERRY DANISHES

serves 4

6 cups flour

½ cup sugar

2 tsp. salt

2 pkgs. rapid rise yeast

½ cup whole milk, warmed

1½ cups half-and-half

4 eggs, lightly beaten

1 can cherry pie filling

2 Tbsp. melted butter for brushing onto danish

ICING DRIZZLE:

1 cup confectioners' sugar

2 Tbsp. milk

½ tsp. vanilla extract

1 In a large bowl, combine flour, sugar, and salt. Cut in butter with a pastry blender until crumbly. Add milk, yeast, half-and-half, and eggs. Stir until mixture forms a soft dough (dough will be sticky). Cover bowl and place in a warm spot for 1 hour or until double in size. Punch down dough. Turn onto a heavily floured surface and divide into 6 portions. Roll each portion into an 18 × 4 rectangle and cut in half to make two strips. Place the two strips side by side and roll each slightly to smooth edges. Starting at one end, twist the two pieces together and shape into a ring, pinching ends together. Place 2 inches apart on greased baking sheets. Repeat with remaining dough. Cover with kitchen towels and let rise in a warm place until doubled, about 45 minutes.

2 Preheat oven to 350 degrees. Using the bottom of a cup, make a ½ inch-deep indentation in the center of each danish. Fill each with ⅓ cup pie filling. Brush dough with melted butter using a pastry brush. Bake 14–16 minutes, or until lightly browned. Remove from pans to wire racks to cool.

3 For icing drizzle: In a small glass measuring cup, mix together sugar, milk, and vanilla until thin and no lumps appear. Drizzle on each cooled danish.

This easy-to-make monkey bread is a winner. The apples caramelize while baking, and the buttery brown sugar syrup that douses the sugared biscuits give this breakfast treat a fall scent and taste that is irresistible. Make this simple recipe for holidays or get-togethers to surprise your guests with something fantastic to start their day.

BAKED APPLE MONKEY BREAD

serves 6–8

½ cup butter

½ cup brown sugar

1¼ cups sugar, divided

½ tsp. vanilla extract

2 pkg. refrigerated biscuits
(I use Pillsbury Grands)

1 Tbsp. cinnamon

2½ cups peeled and chopped fuji apples
(or any sweet baking apple)

1 Preheat oven to 350 degrees. Melt butter in a medium saucepan over medium heat. Stir in brown sugar and ¼ cup sugar. Cook, stirring constantly, 3 minutes or until sugar dissolves. Remove from heat and stir in vanilla.

2 Cut biscuits in half. Stir together cinnamon and remaining 1 cup of sugar in a medium bowl. Add 1 tube of biscuits, cut in half and dredged in sugar mixture on both sides. Arrange coated biscuit pieces in a lightly greased 12-cup Bundt pan and top with chopped apples. Toss remaining biscuits (second tube of biscuits, cut in half) in cinnamon sugar and arrange over apples. Pour butter mixture evenly over biscuits so it reaches every nook and cranny.

3 Place Bundt pan on middle oven rack, and put a foil-lined baking sheet on lower oven rack to catch drippings. Bake for 45 minutes, or until top is golden brown. Let sit in pan for 30 minutes to set. Do not remove while still hot and before monkey bread is set. Carefully invert monkey bread onto a platter, scraping any syrup left in pan over bread. Let cool 10 minutes and serve warm.

I recently made Chocolate Chip Scones for my son's class at school. They were having a Boston tea party and I wanted to make something kid friendly that I knew they would love. What kid would say no to chocolate chips? Adding sparkling sugar, which is a coarse textured sugar, makes them really pop. If you don't have any, regular granulated sugar will do.

CHOCOLATE CHIP SCONES

serves 6

2 cups flour

¼ cup sugar

1 tsp. baking powder

¼ tsp. baking soda

1 stick butter, very cold and diced

1 cup mini chocolate chips

1 cup buttermilk, plus more for brushing

1 tsp. vanilla

course sparkling sugar or granulated sugar for sprinkling

1 Preheat oven to 400 degrees. Line a baking sheet with parchment paper. In a large bowl, whisk together flour, sugar, baking powder, and baking soda. Cut the butter into the flour mixture with a pastry blender or two knives. (The mixture should look like coarse crumbs.) Stir in the chocolate chips. In a small measuring cup, whisk together the buttermilk and vanilla extract and then add to flour mixture. Stir until the dough just comes together. Do not overmix the dough.

2 Transfer dough to a lightly floured surface and knead gently four or five times and. Pat the dough into a circle about 7 inches round and 1½ inches thick. Cut circle in half, then cut each half into 4 triangles. Place scones on the baking sheet. Brush tops of scones with a little milk using a pastry brush and sprinkle with sparkling sugar. Bake for 15–20 minutes, or until lightly golden brown and a toothpick inserted in the middle comes out clean. Remove from oven and place on a wire rack to cool.

TASTY TARTS
AND STRATAS

Always a great choice to serve for holidays and special occasion brunches, because tarts and stratas are just as delicious as they are beautiful.

The secret to bending the apples to create an elegant apple "rose" for this delicious tart is to simply heat the apple slices in the microwave. The slices will become pliable and you can bend them to form a delicate and beautiful french apple rose tart.

FRENCH APPLE ROSE TART

serves 8–10

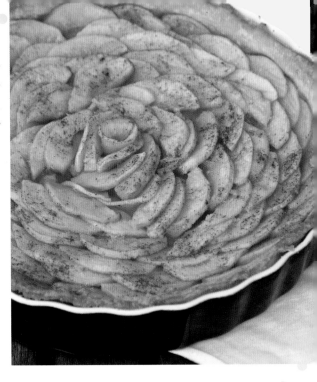

CRUST

2 cups flour

½ tsp. salt

1 tsp. sugar

1½ sticks butter, chilled and diced

½ cup ice cold water

FILLING

4 granny smith apples

½ cup sugar

2-3 Tbsp. cinnamon

4 Tbsp. butter, chilled and diced

1 Preheat oven to 400 degrees. Line tart pan with parchment paper. For crust: Place dry ingredients in the bowl of a food processor fitted with the steel blade. Pulse for a few seconds to combine. Add butter and pulse a few times, until it is in small crumbly bits. While motor is running, pour ice cold water down the feed tube and pulse just until dough starts to come together. You may not need all of the water. You don't want your dough to be too soft and sticky. Place on a floured surface and knead quickly into a ball. Wrap in plastic wrap and chill for 1 hour.

2 Roll dough out to fit the pan you are using. I usually just eyeball this, but if you must measure, just take your pan and place it on top of your dough once rolled to see if it will fit. Trim the edges. Place in the refrigerator to chill while preparing apples.

3 For filling: Peel apples and cut them in half through the stem. Remove stems and cores with a sharp knife. Slice apples crosswise in ¼-inch thick slices. Place slices overlapping around the perimeter of your tart pan and continue until you cannot bend apples enough to place them without gaps (about halfway). Microwave remaining sliced apples for 1 minute or until they are more pliable and soft. This will enable you to bend the apples and finish overlapping them and curl the middle slice to resemble a flower. Sprinkle entire sugar/cinnamon mixture evenly over apples. Place pats of butter all around evenly.

4 Bake for 50–60 minutes, or until crust is browned and edges of apples start to brown. Rotate pan once during cooking. If dough puffs up in one area, simply poke it with a fork or knife. Keep an eye on your tart periodically during baking in case this happens. Let cool to room temperature before cutting.

The vanilla bean cream cheese filling in this tart is so delicious, it's hard to resist grabbing a spoon and eating it straight from the bowl. I use vanilla bean paste because it's less expensive than vanilla beans and has a wonderful, pure vanilla bean taste. You'll still get those amazing little black vanilla bean flecks, which always look gourmet and stunning in desserts.

PEACHES AND CREAM VANILLA BEAN TART

serves 10–12

1 (8-oz.) pkg. cream cheese
⅔ cup sugar
1 tsp. vanilla bean paste
  or vanilla extract
2 Tbsp. sugar
½ tsp. ground cinnamon
2 cups original Bisquick mix
3 Tbsp. shortening
¼ cup butter
⅓ cup milk
1 (21-oz.) can peach pie filling
¼ cup chopped pecans

1 Preheat oven to 400 Degrees. Lightly grease round cookie sheet. In a medium bowl, beat cream cheese, ⅔ cup sugar, and vanilla bean paste or extract with electric mixer on medium speed until smooth. Set aside. In a small bowl, mix 2 tablespoons sugar and cinnamon until combined. Set aside.

2 In large bowl, add bisquick mix. Cut in shortening and butter using a pastry blender until crumbly. Stir in milk. Place dough on surface well sprinkled with Bisquick mix and roll in mix to coat. Knead 8–10 times.

3 Roll out into a 12-inch circle, or slightly larger that your cookie sheet. Place dough on cookie sheet and flatten with dough hanging over edge of pan. Trim edges all around with a knife or scissors. Spread cream cheese mixture onto dough, leaving about ½ inch of space around edge. Add entire can of peach filling to center of tart and spread carefully to edge of cream cheese mixture. Sprinkle pecans over peaches. Starting at the top, take edge of dough and pull down about 4 inches. Do not pull to center of tart. Repeat on all sides. You should have a circle about 5 inches in diameter in the center. Sprinkle sugar and cinnamon onto dough. Bake uncovered for 20 minutes, or until dough is golden brown and is completely cooked through.

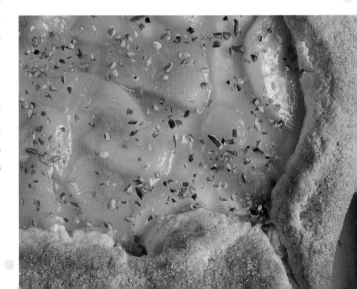

This stunning potato strata has tender soft potatoes and just the right amount of seasoning. It looks fabulous as a main entree for a special occasion breakfast (think mother's day or a bridal brunch) or would work well as a side dish to ham.

POTATO STRATA PIE

serves 8–10

1 Tbsp. extra-virgin olive oil

½ medium onion, thinly sliced

1 red bell pepper, core removed and diced

2 potatoes, peeled and cut into thin slices

sea salt and pepper to taste

8 eggs

2 tsp. chopped fresh or dried rosemary

1 Preheat oven to 400 degrees. Grease a round 10 × 10 quiche dish and set aside. In a large skillet, heat 1 teaspoon oil over medium heat. Add onion and bell pepper, and cook, stirring occasionally, until onion is translucent, about 5 minutes. Transfer to a bowl and set aside.

2 Heat remaining 2 teaspoons oil in skillet. Add potatoes and season generously with salt and pepper. Cook over medium heat, tossing often, until potatoes are tender and lightly browned, about 10 minutes. Combine potatoes in bowl with onion mixture. Place mixture into prepared quiche dish and flatten with a metal spatula.

3 In a large bowl, beat eggs with rosemary, salt, and pepper. Pour over potato mixture and tilt dish to distribute evenly. Bake until set, 15–20 minutes. Cut into wedges and serve.

TASTY TARTS AND STRATAS

If you love Mexican food, you'll love this egg bake with a Mexican twist. It's a hearty breakfast with great spicy flavor thanks to the spicy hot pork sausage. Top with extra cheddar cheese, fresh cilantro, and a dollop of sour cream before serving.

MAKE AHEAD TEX-MEX SAUSAGE STRATA

serves 8–10

1 tube spicy hot pork sausage

3 green onions, sliced

1 can Rotel mexican lime and cilantro diced tomatoes

10 eggs

½ cup sour cream

2½ cups shredded cheddar cheese, divided, plus more for topping

1¼ cups Bisquick mix

salt and pepper to taste

2 Tbsp. fresh cilantro finely chopped or 1 Tbsp. dried cilantro flakes

1 Preheat oven to 350 degrees. Spray a 9 × 13 baking dish with cooking spray. In a frying pan, brown sausage and drain. Add onions and rotel to pan and sauté for 1 minute. In a large bowl, add eggs and sour cream and whisk until combined. Add 1½ cups cheese, Bisquick mix, salt, pepper, and cilantro. Mix well. Add sausage mixture to egg mixture and combine. Add entire mixture to casserole dish and sprinkle with remaining 1 cup cheese. Bake uncovered for 30 minutes or until center is firm to touch.

TIP: Make ahead by preparing filling and pouring into casserole the night before. Cover and refrigerate overnight. Preheat oven in the morning and bake as directed.

If you love rich, strong flavors, you will fall in love with this breakfast pizza. The complex flavors of the gorgonzola cheese and figs are deepened with sweet honey, brown sugared bacon, and caramelized shallots. Tons of flavor, tons of applause!

GORGONZOLA FIG PIZZA

serves 6–8

1 pkg. refrigerated pizza dough

5 pieces bacon

½ cup brown sugar

2 shallots, diced

2 Tbsp. sugar

1 cup crumbled gorgonzola cheese

2 cups chopped dried figs

2 Tbsp. pure honey

1 Preheat oven to 375 degrees. Press refrigerated pizza dough into round cookie sheet. Set aside. Dredge 5 bacon slices in brown sugar and brown in large skillet until fully cooked. Place bacon on paper towel to drain. In a new pan, on medium low heat, cook shallots with sugar until translucent and golden brown, stirring constantly about 7 minutes. Set aside.

2 Sprinkle gorgonzola cheese over pizza dough. Add onions, figs, and bacon. Bake pizza for 15–18 minutes, or until dough is lightly golden brown and fully cooked. Gorgonzola cheese will start to turn a light golden brown color. Remove pizza from oven and drizzle with honey. Slice and serve warm.

I am Italian and love putting Italian flavors in my recipes. Breakfast is no exception. This herbed olive oil crust is flaky and flavorful and becomes the perfect complement to the roasted tomatoes and fresh basil in the filling. I like to sprinkle extra parmesan cheese on top with a light drizzle of extra-virgin olive oil.

HEIRLOOM TOMATO TART WITH HERBED OLIVE OIL CRUST

serves 6–8

CRUST

2 cups whole wheat flour

1 tsp. sea salt

1 tsp. dried basil

1 tsp. dried oregano

¼ cup extra-virgin olive oil

½ cup cold water

FILLING

1 cup spanish onion, diced

1 cup sliced mushrooms

2 Tbsp. butter

4 eggs

⅔ cup milk

1 cup parmesan cheese, shredded

4 Tbsp. fresh basil, chopped

1 garlic clove, pressed in garlic presser

4 large heirloom tomatoes, sliced thin

sea salt and pepper to taste

1 Preheat oven to 350 degrees. In a large bowl, mix flour, salt, and herbs together until combined. Make a well in the center. Add oil and water and mix until just combined and dough forms a ball. On a floured surface, roll out dough 2 inches larger in diameter than your tart pan. I use a standard 9-inch tart pan. Place dough in pan. Prick bottom of tart with fork all around about 10 times. Line with foil and bake the tart shell for 20 minutes. Remove foil and bake until lightly golden brown, about 8 more minutes.

2 For filling: Sauté onion and mushrooms in butter until onions are translucent. In a large bowl, beat eggs and milk until light and fluffy, about 2 minutes. Add remaining ingredients, except tomatoes, and mix well. Pour mixture into prepared tart shell. Layer sliced tomatoes on top, starting from the outer edge and working your way toward the middle. Lightly press tomatoes into egg mixture. Layer remaining tomatoes on top. Sprinkle with salt and pepper and more cheese if desired. Place tart pan on cookie sheet and cover with foil. Bake for 40 minutes on middle rack. Uncover and bake for 30 more minutes, or until center is set and light golden brown.

Using store-bought ready-made pizza dough is a time saver in this easy-to-make breakfast pizza. Be creative with your toppings and add anything that you like. You can have this amazing dish served to your family in less than 20 minutes.

EASY BREAKFAST PIZZA

serves 8–10

1 store-bought 12-inch pizza dough or
    your favorite pizza dough recipe*
olive oil to brush on crust
1 cup shredded mozzarella
1 cup shredded parmesan
3 green onion, chopped
1 tomato, thinly sliced
3 eggs
salt and pepper to taste

1 Preheat oven to 375 degrees. Place ready-made cooked pizza dough on a round cookie sheet of the same size. Brush pizza dough with olive oil.

2 In a small bowl, combine mozzarella and parmesan cheese. Sprinkle dough with ½ of cheese mixture. Evenly spread chopped onions and tomato over the cheese. Carefully break three eggs on top of pizza, being careful to spread them out as much as possible. Add salt and pepper.

3 Bake until cheese bubbles and eggs are fully cooked, about 10–15 minutes. Check if the eggs are done by shaking the cookie sheet. If eggs jiggle, leave in a little longer. Egg yolk does not appear cooked when done baking, but egg whites will no longer be translucent and will turn solid white when cooked. Serve warm.

*If using your own pizza dough recipe: Follow cooking directions for baking pizza dough before adding toppings. Then follow cooking instructions for making breakfast pizza after toppings are applied.

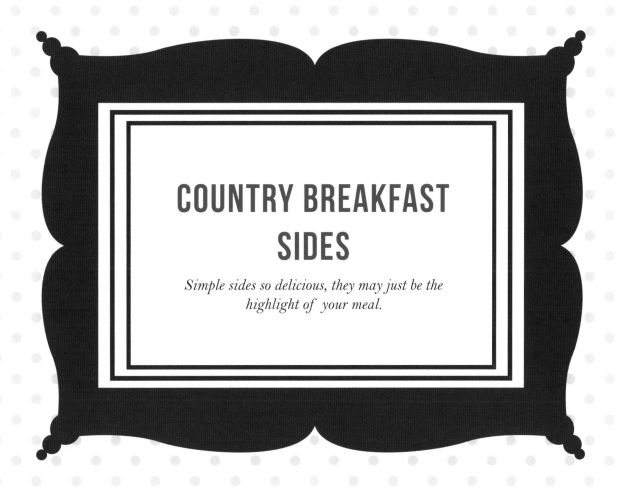

COUNTRY BREAKFAST
SIDES

*Simple sides so delicious, they may just be the
highlight of your meal.*

Quite possibly the most delicious butter ever made. This sweet and sour apple butter is so divine, you can't help but slurp it up straight from the crock-pot. I like to serve mine on toast, bagels with cream cheese, or muffins. Store in a jar with lid and refrigerate to keep on hand when you want a special spread.

CROCK-POT APPLE BUTTER

makes 6 cups

12 apples (I use a mix of golden
    delicious and empire)

⅓ cup sugar

¾ cup brown sugar

1 Tbsp. cinnamon

1 tsp. allspice

1 Tbsp. nutmeg

½ cup water

1 Peel, core, and chop apples. In a crock-pot, add remaining ingredients and stir to combine. Add apples and stir to coat evenly. Adjust crock-pot to medium setting for 6 hours and secure with lid. Stir once about halfway through.

2 When your apples have cooked for 6 hours, stir until you achieve the consistency you are looking for. They will mash up quite nicely at this point, but if you want a purée, place your cooked apple mixture in a food processor or blender and purée until smooth and no lumps appear. Let cool to room temperature and enjoy on toast, bagels, muffins, or crackers. Adjust spices to your liking. Store in sealed container in refrigerator.

Grits are a southern staple for breakfast. This savory recipe has an Italian spin with a hint of garlic and fresh Italian parsley and is topped with a tomato that's roasted to perfection. The half-and-half and cheddar cheese make the grits extra rich and creamy. They are perfect served alone, or even better, with a few sausage links on the side.

BAKED ITALIAN-STYLE CHEESY GRITS

serves 4

1 cup instant grits

2 cups water

2 cups half-and-half

1 cup shredded cheddar cheese, plus 4 Tbsp. for topping

2 cloves of garlic, pressed

1 tsp. sea salt

1 tsp. pepper

¼ cup chopped fresh Italian parsley

1 large beefsteak tomato, sliced

1 Preheat oven to 350 degrees. Prepare 4 ramekins by spraying with olive oil cooking spray or brushing with olive oil. In a medium saucepan, cook grits, water, and half-and-half on medium heat until thickened, 6–7 minutes. Add remaining ingredients (except tomato) and mix well.

2 Divide grits evenly into 4 ramekins. Top each with a single slice of tomato. Sprinkle with more salt and pepper to taste. Add 1 tablespoon of shredded cheeses and a sprig of parsley on top of each tomato. Bake for 7 minutes or until cheese is bubbly and tomato is cooked. Serve warm.

This breakfast side dish is always a hit. It smells so good that my family comes running every time I bake it. The olive oil gives it a wonderful fragrance and flavor, and the cayenne pepper gives it a kick, and the sea salt brings it all home. The potatoes are crunchy on the outside and soft on the inside. We like them as a side dish to eggs and buttered toast.

SPICY OVEN-FRIED POTATOES

serves 8

4 medium to large white potatoes, diced
1 red bell pepper, seeded and chopped
1 large yellow onion, diced
½ cup olive oil
2 Tbsp. Adobo seasoning*
½ tsp. cayenne pepper
1 tsp. oregano
½ tsp. sea salt
½ tsp. black pepper

1 Preheat oven to 400 degrees. Place diced potatoes in a large bowl and cover them with cold water. Allow to soak for 15–20 minutes (or cover and store in refrigerator overnight). Drain the potatoes and pat dry with a paper towel.

2 In a large bowl, combine the potatoes, bell pepper, and onion. Drizzle with olive oil and toss well to coat. In a small bowl, combine the Adobo seasoning, cayenne pepper, oregano, sea salt, and pepper and toss with the potatoes. Spread the potatoes in a thin layer on a rectangular cookie sheet. Bake 30–40 minutes, shaking the pan or using a rubber spatula every 8–10 minutes to ensure all sides of potatoes are deep golden brown.

BAKER'S TIP

Soaking the potatoes removes the starch, enabling the potatoes to bake to a crisp. The longer you soak them, the crispier your potatoes will be.

*Adobo seasoning is an all-purpose seasoning made by Goya. It consists of black pepper, oregano, garlic, and turmeric. If you cannot find Adobo, you may substitute 1 teaspoon of each of these seasonings and omit the ½ teaspoon black pepper called for in the recipe.

There is a reason why the bacon craze became so popular when people started adding it to desserts. There is something about bacon and sugar that tastes heavenly. Cooking the bacon in the oven is a mess-free option, and a time saver, since you can cook the bacon all at once.

SIMPLE SUGARED BACON
serves 4–6

¾ cup brown sugar

3 tsp. cayenne pepper

12 slices thick-cut bacon

1 Preheat oven to 400 degrees. Line a rimmed cookie sheet with parchment paper. In a shallow dish, combine brown sugar and cayenne pepper. Dredge bacon slices in brown sugar mixture, and then arrange bacon on parchment paper, overlapping if necessary to fit all the bacon. Bake until crisp, about 20 minutes, or less if you prefer your bacon less crispy.

The beauty of fall in Virginia is breathtaking, and the comfort foods and bounty available are irresistible. This baked harvest apple recipe is so easy to prepare. Just fill the cored apples with cranberries, butter, spices, and oats and you have yourself a sweet and impressive little breakfast side to start your day any time of the year.

BAKED HARVEST APPLES

makes 4 apples

4 baking apples such as Granny Smith, Fuji, Rome, or Jonagold

1 cup hot water

⅓ cup oats

½ cup brown sugar

1 tsp. cinnamon

¼ tsp. nutmeg

zest and juice of 1 lemon

4 Tbsp. butter

2 Tbsp. dried cranberries

4 Tbsp. butter

1 cup hot water

1 Preheat oven to 375 degrees. Core apples using an apple corer or a sharp knife. Be careful not to poke a hole through the bottom. In a small bowl, mix oats, brown sugar, cinnamon, nutmeg, lemon zest, and cranberries. Stuff each apple with mixture until packed. Squeeze lemon juice evenly over all four apples. Add 1 tablespoon of butter to each, pressing it down into the hole.

2 Place apples in an 8 × 8 baking dish. Add water to dish and bake uncovered for 20–25 minutes, just until they are tender and before they start to split. They will be mushy if overcooked. Let rest for 10 minutes. Sprinkle with extra brown sugar and cinnamon if desired.

Some may not eat sweet potatoes regularly for breakfast, but they love them at special occasions when ham may be served, such as Easter or a special brunch. Roasting diced sweet potatoes with a drizzle of olive oil, fresh rosemary, and a few shakes of sea salt is a rustic, easy side dish, ready in 20 minutes.

ROASTED SWEET POTATOES WITH ROSEMARY

serves 6–8

4 sweet potatoes, peeled and diced
¼ cup olive oil
3-4 fresh sprigs rosemary
sea salt

1 Preheat oven to 400 degrees. Line a large cookie sheet with aluminum foil. Spread diced sweet potatoes evenly on cookie sheet. Drizzle with ¼ cup olive oil or to taste. With your hands, toss the sweet potatoes to coat well. Sprinkle with rosemary and sea salt to taste.

2 Place in middle rack of oven and roast sweet potatoes for 20–30 minutes, or until potatoes are completely tender when pierced with a fork and edges of potatoes are dark brown.

EGGS

Sunny-side up and every which way.

The best thing about breakfast bread bowls is that you can eat the bowl your breakfast is served in. My family thinks they are just as fun to make as they are to eat. Each of my kids likes to stuff their bread bowls with their favorite toppings and cheeses. That way it's made just the way they like it, and everyone eats their breakfast with no complaints.

EASY BREAKFAST BREAD BOWLS

serves 6

6 mini kaiser rolls

2 Tbsp. melted butter

salt and pepper to taste

3 green onions, diced

1 cup pepper jack cheese

1 pint cherry tomatoes, sliced in fourths

½ cup chopped fresh parsley

12 eggs

1 Preheat oven to 350 degrees. With a sharp knife, cut center out of rolls. Scoop out bread from inside using caution not to remove the bottom. Brush inside of roll with melted butter. Sprinkle with salt and pepper. Add 2 tablespoons of toppings (tomatoes, onions, parsley and cheese) inside bread and press firmly, leaving about 1½ inches of space. Crack two eggs on top and sprinkle with more cheese and parsley. Add additional salt and pepper if desired.

2 Bake for 25–30 minutes. Eggs will appear uncooked but will be set. Jiggle pan to check for doneness at 25 minutes. Serve warm.

These savory little bundles are easy to prepare and taste like you spent all morning making them. If you don't want to make your hollandaise sauce from scratch, you can use an instant seasoning packet to save time.

EGGS BENEDICT ASPARAGUS BUNDLES

serves 4–5

1 lb. asparagus, trimmed

8 eggs

salt and pepper

3 Tbsp. olive oil, plus more for frying egg

8-10 slices pancetta

HOLLANDAISE SAUCE

½ cups butter, melted

2 Tbsp. lemon juice

4 Tbsp. hot water

3 egg yolks

dash of cayenne pepper

salt and pepper to taste

1 Preheat oven to 400 degrees. Fill a large pot half full with water and heat over stovetop. Blanch asparagus for 4 minutes. Remove asparagus and lay on paper towels to dry. On a cookie sheet, bunch 5–6 pieces of asparagus together. Wrap each bunch with one piece of pancetta and place with the seam down. Cover with olive oil and salt and pepper to taste. Bake in oven for 12 minutes. Prepare hollandaise sauce.

2 To make hollandaise sauce: Boil about 2 cups of water in the bottom of a double boiler. Reduce the heat to low and let water stop boiling. Place egg yolks in the top of the double boiler and whisk until they begin to thicken. Be sure boiling water is not touching top pan with yolks. Add 1 tablespoon hot water and whisk until sauce begins to thicken. Repeat 3 times. Whisk in lemon juice. Remove from heat and carefully whisk in melted butter. In a small saucepan, fry each egg individually. Remove and transfer to plate. Top each baked asparagus bundle with a fried egg and a drizzle of hollandaise sauce. Add more salt and pepper if needed, and a dash of cayenne pepper.

BAKER'S TIP

Blanching vegetables helps bring out their vibrant natural color, making your asparagus a beautiful bright green. It will cook the vegetable, slightly reducing the amount of time it needs to be in the oven.

This is a light and healthy omelet with wonderful flavor and texture. Baking the eggs reduces the amount of oil or butter you would normally use to fry them on the stovetop. The sour cream keeps the eggs light and fluffy, and using fresh spinach gives you a daily serving of vegetables. The eggs will puff up while baking, and will reduce down once removed from the oven.

BAKED SPINACH OMELET

serves 4–6

4 Tbsp. extra-virgin olive oil

2 cups fresh spinach leaves

10 eggs

¼ cup water

½ cup sour cream

1 garlic clove, crushed

4 Tbsp. chopped chives

salt and pepper to taste

½ cup shredded, reduced-fat mozzarella cheese

1 Preheat oven to 375 degrees. Grease an 8 × 10 casserole dish with cooking spray. In a large sauté pan, drizzle olive oil and on medium high heat, sauté spinach until slightly wilted, about 2 minutes. Remove from heat and set aside.

2 In a large bowl, using a wire whisk, combine eggs, water, sour cream, and crushed garlic until light and fluffy. Small lumps of sour cream will remain. Pour egg mixture into prepared casserole dish. Sprinkle sautéed spinach evenly over egg mixture. Add chopped chives and salt and pepper. Top with mozzarella cheese.

3 Bake for 10 minutes and rotate dish. Bake another 10 minutes, or until egg is set and lightly golden brown on the edges. Be careful not to overbake. Sides will rise first, and egg will continue to rise while baking, but will go down once removed from oven. Serve immediately.

This healthier version of the classic broccoli ham quiche isn't missing anything without the crust. The egg mixture is light and fluffy and the ham, broccoli and cheese bring hearty and satisfying flavors. I like to make this on a lazy Sunday morning and enjoy a slice with a cold glass of orange juice.

CRUSTLESS BROCCOLI AND HAM QUICHE

serves 6–8

6 eggs

¾ cup whipping cream

1 tsp. dried mustard

1 tsp. dried onion flakes or onion seasoning blend

salt and pepper taste

1 cup chopped broccoli, steamed and cooled

1 cup diced cooked ham or deli ham

1 cup shredded cheddar cheese

1 Preheat oven to 350 degrees. Spray a glass pie plate with cooking spray.

2 In a large bowl, beat eggs, whipping cream, dried mustard, dried onion flakes, and salt and pepper with a wire whisk until light and fluffy and fully combined. Stir in broccoli, ham, and cheddar cheese.

3 Pour mixture into prepared pie plate. Bake uncovered for 30 minutes or until egg is puffed and lightly golden brown on the edges and slightly on the top. Egg will flatten once removed from oven. Serve warm and with extra cheese sprinkled on top, if desired.

If you love kalamata olives, this dish is for you. The olives give a burst of flavor to a mellow mushroom frittata that is lightly flavored with garlic, basil, spinach, and parmesan cheese. It's very tasty with orange juice and a side of buttered toast.

OLIVE AND MUSHROOM FRITTATA

serves 8–10

8 eggs

½ cup sour cream

1 tsp. dried basil

1 cup shredded parmesan cheese

½ cup sliced fresh mushrooms

2 Tbsp. olive oil

1 garlic clove, pressed

1 cup frozen spinach, cooked and drained

¾ cup kalamata olives, pitted and sliced in half

salt and pepper to taste

1 Preheat oven to 350 degrees. Spray a standard 9-inch pie dish with cooking spray. In a large bowl, beat eggs, sour cream, dried basil, and shredded parmesan cheese until light and fluffy. Set aside. In a small frying pan, sauté mushrooms in olive oil with crush garlic for 2 minutes on medium heat, until mushrooms are soft and tender. Add sautéed mushrooms, spinach, and olives to egg mixture and mix to combine. Pour egg mixture into prepared pie dish. Sprinkle with salt and pepper. Bake for 20–25 minutes or until middle is set and top is lightly golden brown. Serve warm.

This would be a great Dr. Seuss Day treat for school. Just add green food coloring to the egg mixture and use a mild cheddar cheese. The kids will get a kick out of the fact that the cups are actually made of ham, and they can eat the entire ham and egg cup like a cupcake. Alternately, this would make a great brunch side dish that can be taken as a finger food and eaten by hand.

HAM AND EGG CUPS

serves 4

8 medium slices deli ham

4 large eggs

½ cup shredded pepper jack cheese

1 Tbsp. chopped fresh parsley

salt and pepper to taste

1 Preheat oven to 400 degrees. In a cupcake pan, fit two pieces of ham together in each cupcake cup and press down to take the shape of the pan. Break one egg over ham into cup. Sprinkle with remaining ingredients.

2 Bake for 15 minutes or until whites are completely cooked. Egg yolk will still be runny when broken. Top with extra parsley for a great presentation.

My husband and I make these when we have had one too many muffins and are trying to eat healthy. The avocados serve as bowls for the delicate egg and toppings. Add a squeeze of lime and dash of salt and pepper and you have a fun and healthy way to eat breakfast.

EASY EGGS IN AVOCADO BOWLS

serves 4

2 avocados, ripened

4 eggs

1 small tomato, diced

4 Tbsp. chopped fresh cilantro

1 lime

sour cream (optional)

salt and pepper

1 Preheat oven to 400 degrees. Slice each avocado in half and remove the pits. To lay the avocado evenly on cookie sheet, slice a small level section underneath each avocado. Be careful not to cut through the avocado.

2 With a melon baller or spoon, enlarge the opening of the avocado by removing some of the meat to make room for the egg (about 2–3 scoops). Break open one whole egg in center of each avocado. Sprinkle with salt and pepper and top with diced tomatoes and a tablespoon of cilantro each. Squeeze one lime over all four prepared avocado egg cups.

3 Bake for 15–20 minutes, or until egg whites are cooked and avocado is tender. Add a dollop of sour cream if desired.

This take-and-go veggie and egg muffin is a great addition to your brunch buffet. Add any vegetable and cheese combinations you like and serve with a dash of salt and pepper or hot pepper sauce for the adults.

VEGGIE EGG MUFFINS

makes 12 muffins

½ zucchini, cut in half and julienned

3 large mushrooms, chopped

½ yellow pepper, chopped

2 Tbsp. butter

8 eggs

½ cup sour cream

1 cup shredded cheddar cheese

salt and pepper to taste

hot pepper sauce (optional)

1 Preheat oven to 350 degrees. Spray cupcake pan with cooking spray. In a large skillet sauté vegetables in butter until tender and cooked, about 3 minutes. Remove from heat. In a large bowl, beat eggs and sour cream with wire whisk until light and fluffy and incorporated. Add vegetables, cheese, salt and pepper and mix well. With a ⅓ cup or large spoon, add egg mixture to prepared cupcake pan. Mixture should be about ¾ full. Place pan in center rack and bake for 20 minutes or until set. Insert toothpick in center to determine if fully cooked.

My mom used to make my dad his favorite dinner, stuffed peppers, on special occasions. I thought it would be fun to make this a breakfast version by adding eggs, broccoli, and cheddar cheese to the peppers and roasting them in a nice warm oven until the marvelous scent of roasted peppers permeates through the house. I remember it so well.

OMELET STUFFED PEPPERS

makes 4 peppers

4 large peppers (any color or one of each)

8 eggs

1 cup shredded cheddar cheese

3 Tbsp. sour cream

1 cup finely chopped cooked frozen broccoli

salt and pepper to taste

2 tsp. dried parsley

1 Preheat oven to 350 degrees. Line a medium roasting pan with foil. Spray with cooking spray or drizzle with olive oil. Slice the tops off each pepper and core the center. Be careful not to pierce the bottom of the pepper. If pepper is too slanted, slightly shave off a small even layer on the bottom of the pepper without cutting into the hollow part.

2 In a large bowl, whisk together eggs, cheese, sour cream, broccoli, salt, and pepper until combined and light and fluffy. Pour evenly into prepared peppers. Sprinkle dried parsley evenly over peppers. Cook for 1 hour or until eggs are fully cooked and pepper is tender. Top with extra cheese if desired before serving.

Baking breakfast is a cinch when you throw it all together in individual ramekins and pop it in the oven. The sunny side up egg bakes over the top of cheesy hash browns and the flavors are subtle, light, and tasty.

INDIVIDUAL HASH BROWN AND EGGS

serves 4

1 bag shredded hash browns
½ cup diced yellow onion
2 jalapeños, diced
1 (8-oz.) bag shredded cheddar cheese
1 (10-oz.) can cream of chicken soup
1 cup sour cream
6 eggs
salt and pepper

1 Preheat oven to 375 degrees. Spray 4 ramekins with cooking spray. In a large skillet, prepare hash browns according to package directions. Remove hash browns and in same pan, sauté onions and jalapeño peppers until onion is translucent, 2–3 minutes. Place onions, peppers, and hash browns in a large bowl. Add remaining ingredients and salt and pepper and stir to combine thoroughly. Divide mixture into 4 ramekins, leaving about ½ an inch for the egg. Crack one egg over potato mixture in each ramekin. Sprinkle with a little more salt and pepper.

2 Place ramekins on cookie sheet and bake for 40 minutes or until hash browns are golden brown and egg is fully cooked. You can test the egg for doneness by poking with a fork. It should be solid when done.

NOT YOUR MAMA'S CASSEROLES

Get rid of your old casserole recipe collection and say hello to new and exciting recipes that bring lots of flavor and a fresh new taste to your morning casseroles.

There is something dreamy about bananas and blueberries baking in a warm, sweetened milk bath with fluffy cubed french bread, sprinkled with cinnamon and sugar. A blissful, soft, and delicious bite indeed.

BLUEBERRY BANANA FRENCH TOAST BAKE

serves 8–10

2-3 bananas, sliced

16 oz. soft french bread, cubed

6 eggs

3 cups milk

¼ tsp. nutmeg

2 tsp. cinnamon

pinch of salt

½ cup sugar

1 tsp. vanilla

1 cup fresh blueberries

TOPPING

1 Tbsp. sugar

1 Tbsp. cinnamon

maple syrup for drizzling

1 Preheat oven to 350 degrees. Butter a 9 × 13 casserole dish. Layer sliced bananas on bottom of dish. Place cubed french bread on top of bananas. In a large bowl mix remaining ingredients, except blueberries, with a wire whisk until combined. Pour over bread ensuring each piece is covered. Flip pieces if necessary to soak each one. Press down on bread lightly. In a small bowl mix topping ingredients. Sprinkle with blueberries, tucking in nooks and crannies, and top with cinnamon/ sugar mixture.

2 Bake for 45 minutes or until egg mixture is set and blueberries are bursting and bubbly. Serve warm or at room temperature with maple syrup.

Making individual omelets for 8–10 people would take a lifetime. Now you can serve your omelets to everyone all at once with this delicious casserole that includes toppings for a traditional omelet. Bacon, eggs, sour cream, onions, and cheese are all baked to perfection in this yummy recipe. No sides required here.

COUNTRY OMELET CASSEROLE

serves 8–10

6 strips bacon

18 eggs

½ cup milk

1 cup sour cream

½ cup sliced green onions

1 tsp. salt

1 tsp. pepper

1 cup shredded Swiss cheese

1 cup shredded cheddar cheese

1 Preheat oven to 375 degrees. In a large skillet, cook bacon over medium heat until crisp. Remove and place on paper towel to drain.

2 In a large bowl, beat eggs. Add milk, sour cream, onions, salt, and pepper until light and fluffy. Add cheeses and stir to combine. Pour into a greased 9 × 13 baking dish. Crumble bacon on top.

3 Bake uncovered for 40–45 minutes, or until knife inserted near the center comes out clean. Let stand for 10 minutes before cutting into squares and serving. Top with extra cheese and a dollop of sour cream.

You don't need a fancy crepe pan to make a great crepe. It just takes a well oiled small saucepan and a flick of the wrist. The spinach filling is rich and tasty and the béchamel sauce tops it with wonderful creamy flavor. Use an instant béchamel sauce mix to save time.

SPINACH BREAKFAST CREPES WITH PARMESAN BÉCHAMEL SAUCE

serves 4–6

CREPES

1½ cups milk

3 eggs

1½ cups flour

2 Tbsp. vegetable oil

FILLING

2 cups frozen spinach, cooked and drained

½ lb. bacon, cooked and crumbled, plus extra for topping

1 cup heavy whipping cream

½ cup feta cheese

1½ cups shredded parmesan cheese

salt and pepper

4 eggs, scrambled

BÉCHAMEL SAUCE

5 Tbsp. butter

4 Tbsp. flour

2 cups milk

2 tsp. salt

½ tsp. nutmeg

1 cup parmesan cheese, plus extra for topping

1 Preheat oven to 375 degrees. To make crepes: Grease an 8 × 9 casserole dish. Heat a small nonstick pan and add butter to coat entire pan and up sides. Pour ¼ cup of batter into pan and with a flick of your wrist, swirl quickly to spread evenly, just barely going up the sides of pan. Cook for 30 seconds and flip. Cook another 20 seconds and remove to a wire rack to cool. They need to lay flat and separately in order to work properly when stuffing them. Repeat until all batter is gone.

2 To make filling: In a large bowl, combine spinach, crumbled bacon, whipping cream, feta cheese, and parmesan cheese. Add salt and pepper to taste. Set mixture aside. Scramble eggs in an oiled saucepan and set aside.

3 For béchamel sauce: In a small saucepan, on medium high heat add butter and flour and whisk with a wire whisk to make a roux. Add remaining ingredients and whisk until thickened. Whisk for 3 more minutes or until cheese is melted and mixture is smooth and thickened.

4 To assemble crepes, place 1 cup spinach mixture down the middle of one crepe. Add ¼ cup of scrambled eggs. Sprinkle with extra parmesan cheese. Roll crepe and place seam side down in greased casserole dish. Repeat using all of the spinach mixture.

5 Pour béchamel sauce over crepes in dish. Sprinkle with additional parmesan cheese and crumbled bacon. Bake uncovered for 20 minutes or until edges are lightly golden brown and sauce is bubbly. Serve hot.

Texas toast is a thicker, richer slice of bread that is usually found in the bread section at the grocery store. This sweet orange-flavored french toast can all be baked at once, saving time at the stove making them individually.

GRAND MARNIER FRENCH TOAST —TEXAS STYLE

serves 4

¾ cup half-and-half

2 Tbsp. Grand Marnier
  or 1 Tbsp. orange extract

1 tsp. cinnamon

4 eggs

2 Tbsp. sugar

juice and zest of 1 large orange

dash of salt

8 thick slices Texas-style toast or thick
  sliced bread

confectioners' sugar for dusting

maple syrup

1 Preheat oven to 400 degrees. Lightly grease a large cookie sheet with butter or butter flavored cooking spray.

2 For egg mixture, combine all ingredients up until Texas toast in a large bowl with a wire whisk until thoroughly mixed and fluffy. Dredge each side of sliced Texas toast bread in egg mixture. Place each slice of Texas toast on cookie sheet. Do not let slices touch each other.

3 Bake for 10–12 minutes or until lightly golden brown and toasted. Top with a generous sprinkling of confectioners' sugar, more orange zest, and maple syrup. Serve with orange slices.

This is a complete breakfast in one dish. You have your bacon, eggs, and hash browns all baked to perfection in one flavorful casserole. Add a combination of your favorite cheeses and use good-quality hash browns for best results.

BACON N' EGGS HASH BROWN CASSEROLE

serves 6–8

1 pkg. shredded hash browns

4-5 slices of bacon

1 small onion, diced

6 eggs

2 cups milk

1 Tbsp. dried parsley

2 cups cheddar cheese, or your favorite cheese, divided

salt and pepper to taste

1 Preheat oven to 375 degrees. Lightly spray a 5-quart casserole dish. Prepare hash browns according to package directions. In a large frying pan, fry bacon until crisp and fully cooked. Drain grease from pan. In same pan cook onions. In a large bowl, beat eggs and milk with a wire whisk until light and fluffy. Add hash browns, chopped bacon, parsley, 1 cup cheddar cheese, onion, and salt and pepper. Mix until combined. Pour mixture into prepared casserole dish and top with remaining cheese. Bake uncovered for 40 minutes or until golden and bubbly.

NOT YOUR MAMA'S CASSEROLE

This egg bake has flaky phyllo, tender asparagus, and mushrooms enrobed in a fluffy and delicate eggs that are lightly infused with lemon zest. If you haven't tried lemon with eggs before, you are missing out. It is definitely the hero in this dish, and your guests won't quite know why it's so amazingly delicious until you tell them it's the lemon.

ASPARAGUS AND MUSHROOM PHYLLO BAKE

serves 12–16

1 lb. fresh asparagus

12 eggs

1½ cups shredded parmesan cheese

2 garlic cloves, minced

1 cup sour cream

1 tsp. salt

1 tsp. pepper

zest of one lemon

2 cups fresh mushrooms, rinsed and chopped

1½ sticks butter, melted

16 (14 x 9 inch) sheets phyllo dough

1 Preheat oven to 350 degrees. Grease a 9 × 13 casserole dish and set aside. In a large saucepan, boil water and add sliced asparagus. Cook uncovered for 1 minute or until the asparagus turns bright green. Drain asparagus into a colander and rinse with cold water.

2 In a large bowl, combine eggs, cheese, garlic, sour cream, salt, pepper, and lemon zest. Lightly whisk together until mixture is fully incorporated and light and fluffy. The sour cream will still be lumpy.

3 In prepared casserole dish, unfold phyllo dough and place one sheet into dish. Brush with melted butter. Repeat 7 times using 8 sheets and brushing each with melted butter. Add egg filling. Add another 8 pieces of phyllo dough, brushing each one with melted butter. Trim edges and tuck remaining edges on sides of casserole dish, brushing edges and top of casserole generously with butter.

4 Bake uncovered for 50 minutes or until the phyllo dough is lightly golden brown and firm to the touch. Cool for 20 minutes before cutting. Serve warm.

BAKER'S NOTE

Phyllo dough is very delicate. Use a pastry brush when applying butter, and do so with a light hand. Keep the dough you are not working with moist with a dampened paper towel.

When I first made this dish for breakfast, my husband was the only one who tried it. He ended up eating two helpings and had the rest for dinner that same night. It's that good. Be sure to use the best quality pork sausage you can find. If you don't, your casserole will be overly greasy and not as tasty.

OVERNIGHT PANCAKE SAUSAGE CASSEROLE

serves 6–8

1 lb. bulk pork sausage

10 frozen pancakes

6 eggs

2 cups milk

1 tsp. dry mustard

1 tsp. black pepper

1 tsp. red pepper flakes

½ cup pure maple syrup, plus more for drizzling

1 In a medium skillet, lightly brown sausage, drain. Spray an 8 × 8 casserole dish with cooking spray. Place 5 pancakes on bottom of casserole dish, overlapping the 5th pancake in the middle. Top with half of the cooked sausage.

2 In a medium bowl, beat eggs and next five ingredients with a fork until combined and light and fluffy. Pour half of the egg mixture over pancakes and sausage. Repeat with remaining pancakes, sausage, and egg mixture. Cover with foil and place in refrigerator overnight. In the morning, preheat oven to 375 degrees. Bake covered for 30 minutes. Remove cover and drizzle with maple syrup and bake another 30 minutes, or until top is crispy and egg is cooked through. Serve warm with extra maple syrup if needed.

This healthy breakfast recipe is easy to make and tastes great. For a portable, on-the-go breakfast, fold up the edges of the tortilla before rolling, omit the toppings, and microwave instead of baking.

TURKEY BREAKFAST BURRITOS WITH SALSA

makes 6 burritos

½ lb. ground turkey

1 Tbsp. taco seasoning

1 can Rotel tomatoes with jalapeños

2 Tbsp. butter

6 eggs, lightly beaten

6 large whole wheat tortillas

2 cups cheddar cheese, divided

6 Tbsp. chopped fresh cilantro

1 ripe avocado, diced

1 jar salsa for topping

1 Preheat oven to 400 degrees. In a frying pan, brown turkey until fully cooked. Drain, add taco seasoning and 1 can of rotel with jalapeños, and mix well. Remove turkey from pan and set aside. In same pan, add butter and eggs. Cook eggs for 2–3 minutes, or until fully cooked. Set aside.

2 On each whole wheat tortilla, place about a ¼ cup each of cooked turkey mixture, cheese, and scrambled egg. Sprinkle with cilantro and diced avocados. Roll whole wheat tortilla with mixture inside and place seam down on a lightly greased 9 × 13 casserole dish. Repeat until 6 burritos are completed, and place them touching each other in dish. Top with 1 jar of salsa and remaining cheese. Bake for 15 minutes, or until cheese is bubbly. Serve hot.

It's hard to decide which layer of this smashing casserole is the hero: the tender cake, the sweetened ricotta cheese filling, the sugar and spice topping, or the mixed berry compote. Either way you slice it, this dish is super yummy and is delightful with a cup of coffee and good company.

CHEESE BLINTZ CASSEROLE WITH MIXED BERRY TOPPING

serves 8–10

FILLING

1 (8-oz.) pkg. cream cheese.

½ cup sugar

2 eggs

15 oz. ricotta cheese

zest of 1 lemon

⅛ tsp. salt

1 tsp. vanilla extract

BATTER

1 cup flour

⅓ cup sugar

2 tsp. baking powder

⅛ tsp. salt

2 eggs, lightly beaten

3 Tbsp. butter, melted

3 Tbsp. heavy whipping cream or milk

1 tsp. pure vanilla extract

SUGAR TOPPING

½ cup sugar

½ tsp. baking soda

1 tsp. cinnamon

¼ tsp. nutmeg

BERRY TOPPING

2 cups fresh or frozen mixed berries, blueberries, or raspberries

2 Tbsp. cornstarch

1 Preheat oven to 375 degrees. Lightly spray a 9 × 13 casserole dish with baking spray. For filling: In a mixing bowl, beat cream cheese until light and fluffy, about 2 minutes. Add sugar, eggs, ricotta cheese, lemon, salt, and vanilla and beat for 2 minutes until thoroughly combined and smooth. Set aside.

2 For sugar topping: In a small bowl, combine all ingredients. Set aside.

3 For batter: Sift dry ingredients in a medium bowl. In a small bowl, combine eggs, butter, cream, and vanilla with a wire whisk. Add wet mixture to dry mixture and stir until combined. Pour batter evenly into prepared casserole dish. Pour filling evenly on top of batter. Sprinkle with sugar topping ingredients.

4 Bake uncovered for 45–50 minutes or until toothpick inserted into center of casserole comes out clean. While baking, prepare berry topping. In a small saucepan on medium heat, stir mixed berries with cornstarch. Stir thoroughly until thickened and cornstarch is fully incorporated, about 5 minutes. Once casserole is room temperature, slice into squares and spoon berry topping over top before serving.

I made this recipe on our first Christmas in our new home. My daughter loved it so much that it became a tradition to make it every year for Christmas morning breakfast. I assemble it on the night before and pop it in the oven before waking the kids up. Once they are done opening their presents, the casserole is baked and ready to eat.

OVERNIGHT PECAN FRENCH TOAST CASSEROLE

serves 8–10

1 loaf soft french bread, sliced (about 20 1-inch slices)

6 eggs

1½ cups half-and-half

2 cups milk

3 Tbsp. sugar

1 tsp. vanilla extract

1 tsp. cinnamon

½ tsp. nutmeg

PRALINE TOPPING

1½ sticks butter, softened

¾ cup brown sugar

1 cup chopped pecans

2 Tbsp. light corn syrup

½ tsp. cinnamon

½ tsp. nutmeg

maple syrup (optional)

1 Arrange bread slices in a buttered 9 × 13 casserole dish in 2 rows, overlapping the slices. In a large bowl, combine eggs, half-and-half, milk, sugar, vanilla, cinnamon, and nutmeg and whisk until blended but not too bubbly. Pour mixture over the bread slices, making sure all pieces are covered evenly. Cover with foil and refrigerate overnight.

2 The next day, preheat oven to 350 degrees. Make praline topping by combining all ingredients, except maple syrup, in a medium bowl and mixing well. Spread praline topping evenly over the bread and bake for 45 minutes, until puffed and lightly golden. Serve with maple syrup if desired.

BAKER'S NOTE

We omit the pecans since my daughter has developed an allergy to tree nuts. Skip the nuts if you need to, and it will be just as tasty.

PANCAKES

On the flip side . . . dessert-inspired pancakes!

Have your loved one wake up to a fun stack of cake batter sprinkles pancakes drizzled with warmed frosting and topped with a birthday candle. Go ahead and sing your heart and start the day with smiles, love, and laughter, all while making a delicious memory.

SPRINKLES BIRTHDAY PANCAKES

serves 4–6

2 cups flour

1 cup yellow cake mix

1 tsp. baking powder

½ tsp. baking soda

¼ tsp. salt

2 cups buttermilk

1½ cups milk

1 tsp. pure vanilla extract

2 Tbsp. vegetable oil

½ cup rainbow sprinkles, plus more for topping

1 can icing

1 Preheat a large griddle to medium heat. Butter griddle generously or spray with butter-flavored cooking spray. Mix dry ingredients with a wire whisk. Add all wet ingredients and mix until just combined. Mixture will be a little lumpy. Add sprinkles to batter and mix gently.

2 With a measuring cup, pour ½ cup of batter onto heated griddle. For a large griddle you should be able to cook three pancakes at a time. In 1–2 minutes, bubbles should start to form on top of the pancake. Flip once this happens. Cook for 1 minute longer and, using a spatula, transfer pancake to a cookie rack to cool slightly. Repeat until all pancakes are cooked.

3 Remove lid and foil from frosting can. Microwave on medium-high heat for 15 seconds. Stir. Mixture should be thinned and slightly warmed. If not, microwave for a few more seconds but be careful not to overheat. Mix well and using a spoon pour icing onto pancakes and top with more sprinkles.

This recipe is special to me because I came up with it for my dad. His favorite dessert is pecan pie, so I knew I wanted to include a pecan pie–inspired breakfast in my cookbook. The butter-flavored pancakes are made with southern pecan coffee creamer instead of milk to give it extra pecan pie flavor, and the topping is sweet and buttery with rich butterscotch notes just like the actual pie. Top with bits of bacon for an authentic breakfast garnish, and because salty and sweet can't be beat!

PECAN PIE PANCAKES

serves 4–6

⅓ cup sugar

2 cups flour

1 tsp. baking powder

1 tsp. baking soda

1 egg

2 cups liquid Southern pecan
   coffee creamer

2 Tbsp. vegetable oil

1 tsp. vanilla

1 cup chopped pecans

1 In a large bowl, combine dry ingredients with wire whisk. In a separate small bowl whisk egg, coffee creamer, vegetable oil, and vanilla until light and fluffy, about 2 minutes. Add wet ingredients to dry ingredients mixture and fold until just combined. Do not overmix.

2 Preheat griddle to medium-high heat and add butter. With a ¼ cup, add batter to greased griddle and sprinkle with about 1 tablespoon pecans. Flip once bubbles form on top of pancake. Cook another 1 minute or until completely cooked or lightly golden brown. Allow to cool slightly on wire cookie rack.

BAKER'S TIP:

Adding the pecans to the pancake before flipping instead of directly in the batter will result in toasting the pecans directly on the griddle, bringing out the nutty flavor.

Dessert doesn't have to be at the end of the day. Start your morning with a breakfast that tastes just like blueberry pie, but even better. The buttermilk pancakes are light and tender, with just a hint of lemon. The blueberry compote is sinfully delicious, and tastes just like sweet blueberry pie filling. These are literally the best pancakes I have ever tasted.

BLUEBERRY PIE PANCAKES

serves 4–6

1¼ cups flour

1 Tbsp. sugar

1 tsp. baking powder

¼ tsp. baking soda

pinch of salt

1 tsp. cinnamon

2 eggs, lightly beaten

1½ cups buttermilk

1 tsp. vanilla extract

zest and juice of 1 lemon

BLUEBERRY COMPOTE

1 cup water

2 Tbsp. cornstarch

1 pint blueberries

¼ cup sugar

1 Preheat an electric griddle to medium-high heat. In a large bowl, mix together all dry ingredients. In a separate small bowl, whisk together all wet ingredients until light and fluffy and well combined. Stir in juice and zest of 1 lemon. Add wet mixture into bowl of dry ingredients and lightly fold mixture together until just combined. Do not overmix.

2 Using a ¼ measuring cup, add pancake batter to hot griddle and turn once bubbles start to form, about 2 minutes, depending on how hot your griddle is. If griddle is smoking and edges are starting to burn, your griddle is too hot. Once flipped, cook pancake for 1 more minute or until fully cooked. Lay on wire rack to cool slightly. Do not stack pancakes on top of each other once off the griddle. This will make them mushy and continue cooking them. Make compote and add on top of stacked pancakes.

3 To make compote: In a small measuring cup, mix together water and cornstarch until cornstarch is fully absorbed. In a small saucepan, on medium-high heat, add blueberries, sugar, and water/cornstarch and stirring constantly until blueberries start to burst and mixture coats the back of spoon and thickens.

This recipe brings me back to when I was a little girl. I loved fresh strawberries and whipped cream, and I often asked my mom to make strawberry shortcake for dessert. This stack of pancakes taste so much like the real thing that it sends me down memory lane of summer's in Burke, VA, just being a kid and loving life.

STRAWBERRY SHORTCAKE PANCAKES WITH HONEY

serves 4–6

⅓ cup sugar

2 cups flour

1 tsp. baking powder

1 tsp. baking soda

¼ tsp. nutmeg

1 egg

2 cups milk

2 Tbsp. vegetable oil

1 tsp. vanilla

1 quart strawberries, washed and sliced

fresh whipped cream or frozen whipped topping

honey for drizzling

1 In a large bowl, combine dry ingredients with a wire whisk. In a separate small bowl, whisk egg, milk, vegetable oil, and vanilla until light and fluffy, about 2 minutes. Add wet ingredients to dry ingredients and fold until just combined. Do not overmix.

2 Preheat griddle to medium-high heat and add butter. With a ¼ cup, add batter to greased griddle and flip once bubbles form on top of each pancake. Cook another minute, or until completely cooked or lightly golden brown. Allow to cool slightly on wire cookie rack. Top with sliced strawberries, whipped cream, and honey before serving.

You don't need a flame to appreciate good bananas foster flavor. These pancakes have the same rich, caramelized, buttery flavor as the popular dessert that originated from a restaurant called Brennan's in New Orleans. My youngest son is named Brennen, and even though he is not a huge banana eater, I dedicate this recipe to him.

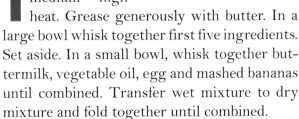

BANANAS FOSTER PANCAKES

serves 4–6

2 cups flour

2 tsp. sugar

2 tsp. baking powder

⅛ tsp. nutmeg

¼ tsp. salt

2½ cups buttermilk

2 Tbsp. vegetable oil

1 large egg

2 bananas, mashed

TOPPING SYRUP

½ cup butter

¼ cup brown sugar

1 tsp. cinnamon

¼ tsp. nutmeg

½ cup maple syrup

1 tsp. rum extract

4 bananas, sliced

1 Preheat large griddle to medium high heat. Grease generously with butter. In a large bowl whisk together first five ingredients. Set aside. In a small bowl, whisk together buttermilk, vegetable oil, egg and mashed bananas until combined. Transfer wet mixture to dry mixture and fold together until combined.

2 Using a ¼ cup measuring cup, scoop batter onto prepared griddle. Once bubbles start to form, flip pancake and cook for another minute until lightly golden brown and cooked through. Do not overcook. Place cooked pancakes on wire rack to cool slightly. Top with prepare topping syrup and sliced bananas.

3 For topping: In a large skillet, mix butter, brown sugar, cinnamon, nutmeg, maple syrup and rum extract. Cook mixture over medium-high heat 2–3 minutes, stirring constantly, until sugar dissolves and mixture is thick. Reduce heat to medium and add bananas and stir gently covering all bananas. Cook about 3 minutes, or until bananas are glossy and coated with sauce.

When I first made these for my kids, they were not sure about eating red pancakes. But once they tasted the cocoa flavor and sweetened cream cheese icing, they were hooked. They asked for more, with lots of frosting and a side of strawberry milk to wash it all down.

RED VELVET PANCAKES WITH MAPLE CREAM CHEESE FROSTING

serves 4–6

2 cups flour

3 Tbsp. cocoa powder

½ tsp. baking soda

1½ tsp. baking powder

2 cups buttermilk

⅓ cup sugar

1 Tbsp. white vinegar

2 eggs

2 Tbsp. red food coloring

2 tsp. vanilla extract

2 Tbsp. vegetable oil

FROSTING

1 (8-oz.) pkg. cream cheese, softened

2 Tbsp. maple syrup

1 tsp. vanilla extract

1½ cups confectioners' sugar

1 Preheat an electric nonstick griddle to medium-low heat. In a mixing bowl, whisk together flour, cocoa powder, baking soda, and baking powder. Set aside.

2 In a liquid measuring cup, add buttermilk, sugar, vinegar, eggs, food coloring, vanilla, and vegetable oil and whisk until fluffy and well combined. Slowly add wet ingredients to dry ingredients and mix until just combined. Do not overmix batter.

3 Butter the griddle generously and pour about a ¼–⅓ cup batter at a time onto the hot griddle. Cook until bubbles begin to appear on the top surface of the pancakes then flip and cook opposite side until pancake is cooked through but before they turn golden brown. Check doneness by using a spatula and gently lifting the underside of the pancake. Mix together frosting ingredients. Drizzle a stack with frosting or lightly spread each pancake with the icing.

Chocolate and peanut butter go together like peas and carrots. I am sure you have had the delectable combo, but have you ever had chocolate peanut butter spread with bananas? These pancakes are made with chocolate silk which is then smeared onto each pancake topped with sliced bananas and doused in maple syrup. Scrumptious!

CHOCOLATE SILK AND BANANA PANCAKES

serves 4–6

1½ cups flour

2½ tsp. baking powder

2 Tbsp. sugar

½ cup chocolate peanut butter spread, plus more for topping

2 Tbsp. butter, melted

2 large eggs, lightly beaten

1½ cups buttermilk

2 bananas, sliced.

1 Preheat griddle to medium-high heat. Add butter and melt. In a large bowl, combine flour, baking powder, and sugar. Set aside. In a medium bowl, whisk together peanut butter and butter until smooth. Add eggs and buttermilk and stir until combined. Add more buttermilk if mixture is too thick. Combine with dry ingredients.

2 Using a ¼ cup measuring cup, add batter to prepared griddle. Once bubbles start to form and edges are light golden brown, flip pancake and cook another minute. Do not press pancake. When pancakes is cooked through and not too brown, transfer to a wire rack until you are finished making the rest of the pancakes. Add sliced bananas and a smear of chocolate peanut butter spread before serving.

A favorite in the fall, but so they are delicious that we make them year round. Buttermilk and pumpkin go beautifully together, making a moist and fluffy pancake spiced with the flavors of fall and a hint of pumpkin. Stack 'em high and slather with butter and syrup!

PUMPKIN PIE PANCAKES
serves 4–6

1¼ cups flour

2 Tbsp. sugar

2 tsp. baking powder

½ tsp. cinnamon

½ tsp. ground ginger

½ tsp. salt

⅛ tsp. nutmeg

1 tsp. cloves

1½ cups buttermilk

6 Tbsp. canned pumpkin purée

2 Tbsp. butter, melted

1 egg

maple syrup for drizzling

1 Preheat a griddle on medium heat. Slather the entire surface with butter and melt. Whisk together dry ingredients. In a separate bowl, stir together buttermilk, pumpkin purée, melted butter, and egg until combined. Fold mixture into dry ingredients.

2 On prepared griddle, pour ¼ cup batter for each pancake. I use a measuring cup for this. Cook pancakes about 2–3 minutes per side or until light golden brown. Cool on wire rack for a few minutes before stacking pancakes. Serve with butter and syrup.

DESSERTS

Breakfast-inspired after-dinner sweets.

My neighbors absolutely loved this cake and so did we. The oats give the cake an unusual but pleasant texture and taste, and adds moistness to the cake that makes it irresistible. The maple cream cheese frosting goes beautifully with this cake because it complements the cinnamon and brown sugar. Introduce this cake to your family and they will request it often.

BROWN SUGAR OATMEAL CAKE WITH MAPLE CREAM CHEESE FROSTING

serves 8–10

CROWELL

1 cup boiling water

1 cup quick cooking oats

1 stick butter

1 cup brown sugar

½ cup granulated sugar

3 eggs

¼ cup sour cream

1 tsp. vanilla extract

2 cups flour

2 tsp. baking powder

1 tsp. cinnamon

½ tsp. baking soda

½ tsp. nutmeg

MAPLE CREAM CHEESE FROSTING

1 cup butter

1 (8-oz.) pkg. cream cheese

½ cup brown sugar

½ cup pure maple syrup

3 tsp. vanilla

pinch of salt

4 cups confectioners' sugar

1 Preheat oven to 350. Spray two 8-inch round cake pans with baking spray made with flour. In a small bowl, pour boiling water over oats; let stand 10 minutes. In a mixing bowl, beat butter and sugars until fluffy, about 2 minutes.

2 Add eggs, one at a time, beating well after each addition and scraping sides of bowl. Beat in sour cream and vanilla. In a separate bowl, combine flour, baking powder, cinnamon, baking soda and nutmeg. Add to creamed mixture ½ cup at a time on low speed. Stir in oats.

3 Pour batter into prepared cake pans. Bake for 25 minutes, or until center springs back when touched. Place cake pans on wire rack and cool for 30 minutes in pan. Then remove cakes from pan and place on wire racks to cool completely before frosting.

4 To make frosting: In a large bowl, beat butter and cream cheese until light and fluffy, about 5 minutes. Add remaining ingredients, except confectioners' sugar, and mix until combined. Add confectioners' sugar 1 cup at a time on low speed. Scrape sides. Beat on high for 1 minute. Repeat until all sugar is added. Frost cooled cake and serve.

I have to admit, this fluffy, flavorful buttercream is spot on. It tastes just like Fruity Pebbles cereal with hints of orange, lemon, vanilla, and maraschino cherry flavors. It's a fun, kid-friendly cupcake that has Fruity Pebbles mixed right into the batter and also used as a colorful and tasty topping. I serve them to my kids as an after school treat and they were are in seconds.

FRUITY PEBBLES CUPCAKES

makes 18 cupcakes

CUPCAKES

1 box strawberry cake mix, prepared according to box directions

1 cup Fruity Pebbles cereal, plus extra for topping

BUTTERCREAM ICING

4 sticks butter

5 cups confectioners' sugar

1 Tbsp. pure orange extract

1 Tbsp. pure lemon extract

1 tsp. pure vanilla extract

1 Tbsp. maraschino cherry juice

1 For cupcakes: Preheat oven to 350 degrees. Line cupcake pans with cupcake liners and set aside. In an electric mixer, on low speed, prepare cake mix according to box directions, mixing for 2 minutes. Add Fruity Pebbles and stir until combined. Using a large cookie scoop, add 1 scoop of batter to each cupcake liner. Bake for 18 minutes, or until center comes out clean when a toothpick is inserted and top is firm to the touch. Let cool on wire rack completely.

2 For icing: In an electric mixer, beat the butter until light and fluffy, about 5 minutes. Add confectioners' sugar a ½ cup at a time on low speed. Increase speed to high and beat for 1 minute. Repeat until all sugar is added. On low speed, add extracts and cherry juice until fully combined.

3 Using a large pastry bag and Wilton 2A tip, pipe a ring around the outer edge of a cupcake. Dip iced cupcake into fruity pebbles, twisting your wrist as you go around the cupcake gently. Pipe a mound of icing in the center of the cupcake and top with a maraschino cherry. Repeat for all cupcakes.

Substituting Cinnamon Toast Crunch cereal for Rice Krispie Treats gives this classic recipe an exciting new twist. The sweet, creamy marshmallow flavor tastes amazing with a hint of cinnamon and the buttery flavor in each bite compliments the Cinnamon Toast Crunch cereal giving it a totally scrumptious flavor.

CINNAMON TOAST CRUNCH BARS

serves 4–6

¼ cup butter
1 bag large marshmallows
  (about 4 cups)
¼ tsp. cinnamon
5-6 cups Cinnamon Toast Crunch cereal

1 In large saucepan, melt butter, marshmallows, and cinnamon on low/medium heat until smooth and there are no lumps. Put Cinnamon Toast Crunch cereal in a large bowl. Pour marshmallow mixture over cereal and gently combine, coating all cereal.

2 Butter or lightly spray an 8 × 8 casserole dish. Pour cereal mixture into dish and press lightly with your hands. If cereal is sticking to your hands, butter your hands lightly and, with swift motion, press down on cereal until it is level and packed in. Cover and let sit for an hour. You may also place in refrigerator to set faster. Once completely set and solid, cut into squares.

This bread pudding not only became a hit at the Bakehouse, but with my neighbors too. Some said it was the best bread pudding they have ever tasted. Others said they don't typically like bread pudding, but this one was really delicious. I agree with them 100%, and the best part is that it tasted even better the next day. This is the dessert that keeps on giving!

CINNAMON SWIRL BREAD PUDDING WITH RASPBERRIES

serves 8–10

16 slices cinnamon swirl bread

butter for bread, softened

6 eggs

1 cup whipping cream or half-and-half

3 cups milk

⅔ cup sugar

½ tsp. cinnamon

1 tsp. vanilla

confectioners' sugar for dusting

1 cup fresh raspberries

1 Preheat oven to 350. Butter a 9 × 13 baking dish. Do not use baking spray or cooking spray. Butter 16 slices of cinnamon swirl bread and cut diagonally. Place each piece in baking dish, buttered side up with the pointed end at the top. Overlap each piece.

2 In a large bowl, with a wire whisk, beat eggs, whipping cream, milk, sugar, cinnamon, and vanilla until combined. Pour mixture over bread slices, saturating each piece and moving the pieces slightly to drench. Press down on bread lightly to submerge top of bread. Cover and refrigerate for an hour.

3 Bake for 30 minutes or until custard is set and bread is light golden brown and firm to the touch. Sprinkle with raspberries. Remove from oven and cover. Let come to room temperature on counter. Sprinkle with confectioners' sugar and serve.

This recipe was developed on accident. I was making marbled banana bread and added too much batter to the loaf pan, and it overflowed while baking. The scent was heavenly and I knew it would still taste delicious, so I let it finish baking instead of throwing it out. I cut the ugly loaf of bread into cubes and made a fabulous chocolate bread pudding that turned out to be completely out of this world. The lesson I learned was to never throw away your mess-ups.

MARBLED CHOCOLATE BANANA BREAD PUDDING

makes 2 loaves of banana bread and 1 batch of chocolate bread pudding, serves 6–8

BANANA BREAD

3 cups flour

½ tsp. baking soda

½ tsp. baking powder

2 cups sugar

4 ripe bananas

½ cup melted butter

2 eggs

1 cup buttermilk

1 tsp. vanilla extract

PUDDING

4 eggs

1 cup of milk

1 cup heavy cream

½ cup sugar

2 tsp. rum extract

2 tsp. vanilla extract

2 Tbsp. cocoa powder

CHOCOLATE BANANA BREAD

½ cup cocoa powder such as Hershey's (mixed into 2 cups prepared banana bread batter)

1 Preheat oven to 350 degrees. Prepare two standard loaf pans by spraying with baking spray. In a large bowl, sift flour, baking soda, and baking powder. In a medium bowl, mash bananas with a fork until only small chunks appear. Add melted butter, sugar, eggs, buttermilk, and vanilla and mix well with a wire whisk. Add wet ingredients to dry ingredients. Fold until combined. Do not overmix. In a small bowl remove 2 cups of banana bread batter and add ½ cup of cocoa powder. Mix well.

2 In 1 loaf pan, add 1 cup banana batter. Then add 1 cup of chocolate batter over top. Add 1–1½ more cups of banana mixture on top. With a knife, swirl through mixtures to create a marble effect. Repeat with second loaf pan. Fill only a little over half way in loaf pans. If any batter remains, bake in a tiny loaf or muffin tin. Bake for 1 hour or until the middle of each loaf comes out clean when a toothpick is inserted. Moist crumbs will stick to toothpick.

3 For pudding: Mix all ingredients together until well combined. Once bread is baked and cooled, slice it into small squares. Spray a medium-size casserole dish with baking spray. Lay bread cubes in dish and pour pudding mixture over bread. Cover and let soak in refrigerator for at least an hour or overnight. Be sure to cover each piece. Bake at 350 degrees for 45 minutes or until egg mixture is cooked through. Serve warm.

BAKER'S TIP:

Bake bread the day before, and then assemble bread pudding, cover, and store in refrigerator. Bake the next morning for a delightful breakfast treat.

We always bake banana bread for Thanksgiving and put it on the dessert table with all the wonderful baked goods. This banana cake is a bit lighter in texture than standard banana bread, and it's baked in a bundt pan, which makes it totally dessert worthy. Sprinkle with confectioners' sugar to make it look pretty before serving.

BANANA BUNDT CAKE

serves 8–10

3 cups flour

2 tsp. baking soda

½ tsp. salt

2 sticks butter, room temperature

2 cups sugar

2 tsp. vanilla extract

2 eggs

4 very ripe bananas, mashed

1 cup sour cream

confectioners' sugar for sprinkling

1 Preheat to 350 degrees and move rack to center. Generously butter or spray a Bundt pan. Whisk flour, baking soda, and salt together. With an electric mixer fitted with a paddle attachment, beat the butter until creamy. Add sugar and beat at medium speed until pale and fluffy. Beat in vanilla, then add eggs one at a time. Reduce mixer speed to low and mix in bananas. Mix in half the dry ingredients (batter will curdle) and sour cream, then rest of flour mixture. Scrape batter into pan and level with a spatula.

2 Bake for 45–60 minutes, checking every 5 minutes after it's baked for 45 minutes and cake is browned on the edges. Transfer cake to a rack and cool for 10 minutes before unmolding onto the rack to cool to room temperature. If you have time, wrap cooled cake in plastic and allow it to sit overnight before serving—it's even better the next day.

My late grandmother use to make oatmeal taste like homemade vanilla pudding. I always asked for it when I spent the night as a child. She never wrote her recipes down, but I think I came up with something close and equally delicious. It's a light and creamy vanilla oatmeal with the added twist of a crunchy sweet crème brûlée topping.

CRÈME BRÛLÉE VANILLA OATMEAL

Serves 4

6 cups milk, divided

2 cups quick oats

½ cup sugar

1 tsp. vanilla extract or vanilla
  bean paste

1 tsp. cinnamon

⅛ tsp. nutmeg

2 egg whites

1 cup sugar for topping

kitchen torch

1 In a large saucepan, combine 4 cups milk with oats. Stir on medium-low heat for about 10 minutes. Add sugar, vanilla, cinnamon, and nutmeg and stir to combine. Add egg whites, stirring vigorously until mixture begins to boil. Pay close attention to whipping the egg whites. Once boiling, add two remaining cups of milk and stir until thickened. Remove from heat. Pour into 4 prepared ramekins. Pour oatmeal into prepared dish.

2 For crème brûlée: Sprinkle enough sugar over top of each ramekin to cover completely. Using a standard kitchen torch, torch the sugar on high heat until melted and golden brown.

BAKER'S NOTE:

If desired, skip crème brûlée step and sprinkle oatmeal with brown sugar and cinnamon.

I love bread pudding for breakfast, and this one is so sweet and full of caramel flavor that I think it is wonderful for dessert. The sea salt is a popular choice to bring out the delicious caramel flavor. It's moist and rich like traditional bread puddings, and is truly decadent.

OVERNIGHT SALTED CARAMEL BREAD PUDDING

serves 8–10

1 (13-16-oz.) loaf French bread

butter for pan

8 eggs

2 cups half-and-half

1 cup milk

2 Tbsp. sugar

1 tsp. vanilla extract

½ tsp. cinnamon

½ tsp. nutmeg

PRALINE TOPPING

2 sticks butter

1 cup brown sugar

2 Tbsp. caramel topping,
    more for drizzling (optional)

½ tsp. cinnamon

½ tsp. nutmeg

dash of sea salt

dash of confectioners' sugar (optional)

1 The next day, preheat oven to 350 degrees. Spread praline topping evenly over the bread or on each slice and bake for 45 minutes, until puffed and light golden. Cool for 10 minutes and drizzle with caramel topping and a sprinkling of sea salt and confectioners' sugar.

2 Slice french bread into 20 slices, 1 inch thick each. Arrange slices in a generously buttered 9 × 13 casserole dish in 2 or 3 rows. You can overlap the slices if necessary. In a large bowl, combine eggs, half-and-half, milk, sugar, vanilla, cinnamon, and nutmeg, and beat with a whisk until blended but not too bubbly. Pour mixture over the bread slices, making sure all are covered evenly with milk/egg mixture. Flip each slice of bread to ensure fully soaked. Spoon some mixture in between the slices. Cover with foil and refrigerate overnight.

3 For the praline topping: Combine all ingredients in a medium bowl and blend well. Spread over bread as directed.

INDEX

COOKING MEASUREMENT EQUIVALENTS

Cups	Tablespoons	Fluid Ounces
⅛ cup	2 Tbsp.	1 fl. oz.
¼ cup	4 Tbsp.	2 fl. oz.
⅓ cup	5 Tbsp. + 1 tsp.	
½ cup	8 Tbsp.	4 fl. oz.
⅔ cup	10 Tbsp. + 2 tsp.	
¾ cup	12 Tbsp.	6 fl. oz.
1 cup	16 Tbsp.	8 fl. oz.

Volume Equivalents

Cups	Fluid Ounces	Pints/Quarts/Gallons
1 cup	8 fl. oz.	½ pint
2 cups	16 fl. oz.	1 pint = ½ quart
3 cups	24 fl. oz.	1½ pints
4 cups	32 fl. oz.	2 pints = 1 quart
8 cups	64 fl. oz.	2 quarts = ½ gallon
16 cups	128 fl. oz.	4 quarts = 1 gallon

Other Helpful Equivalents

1 Tbsp	3 tsp.
8 oz.	½ lb.
16 oz.	1 lb.

METRIC MEASUREMENT EQUIVALENTS

Approximate Weight Equivalents

Ounces	Pounds	Grams
4 oz.	¼ lb.	113 g
5 oz.		142 g
6 oz.		170 g
8 oz.	½ lb.	227 g
9 oz.		255 g
12 oz.	¾ lb.	340 g
16 oz.	1 lb.	454 g

Approximate Volume Equivalents

Cups	US Fluid Ounces	Milliliters
⅛ cup	1 fl. oz.	30 mL
¼ cup	2 fl. oz.	59 mL
½ cup	4 fl. oz.	118 mL
¾ cup	6 fl. oz.	177 mL
1 cup	8 fl. oz.	237 mL

Other Helpful Equivalents

½ tsp.	2½ mL
1 tsp.	5 mL
1 Tbsp.	15 mL

AUTHOR BIOGRAPHY

Dina Foglio Crowell is a proud military wife, mother, baker, and blogger. She is the author, recipe developer, photographer, and food stylist behind the popular baking blog, *Buttercream Bakehouse*. Dina is a self-taught baker and an award-winning cake decorator with two second place wins at the National Capital Area Cake Show.

Her passion for baking and cake decorating led her to open a home-based custom cake business in 2009 called Buttercream. She soon embarked on sharing her sought-after recipes and created a baking blog in 2010 called *Buttercream Bakehouse*, which soon became her full-time passion.

As her blog grew in popularity, she was accepted by dozens of ad networks including Pollinate Media Group and Collective Bias, and as a freelance writer for Tap Influence and a brand ambassador for well-known brands including Hershey's, Nestle, Kraft Foods and Betty Crocker. She spends her free time as a volunteer field editor for *Taste of Home Magazine* and is listed as a favorite blog at *www.tasteofhome.com*.

Her biggest cheerleaders are her parents, Lucy and Jimmy Foglio, who continue to inspire her to work hard every day and to reach for the stars. She currently lives in the suburbs of Fredericksburg, Virginia with her husband and her four beautiful children. For fun she likes to cook for her husband John, cheer on her two youngest sons Brennen and Kayeden in baseball, volunteer in their schools, shop with her teenage daughter Ashlynn, and have one-on-one talks with her oldest son, Tristen. The family also has two Maltese, named Oliver Nutmeg and Finnegan Chestnut.